I, Jack Cuthrell w
that originally wr
That is a fact.

But, the thoughts, were given to me, (inspired, if you wish) by four voices within my mind.

Four voices that were and are, very warm, very beautiful personalities. These "voices"have expressed knowledge beyond my knowledge, wisdom beyond my abilities, Love of a greater source, than I can even comprehend.

These voices have names.

TIM: A father figure and a dear friend, that has changed my life, and me.

SAM: A poor artist that lived in Brooklyn, and has used my hand to draw of his life.

RUTH: Sam's beloved wife, that tells of her life, their son, and her beliefs.

DOT: My sister, who died in 1994, and still picks on me, but big sisters do that.

I

LETTERS OF THE SOUL

from the

SILENCE OF THE MIND

by

JACK CUTHRELL

SPIRITUAL QUEST

Tequesta, Florida

III

To respect privacy, the names of some people have been changed. Similarities to other people living or deceased are unintentional.

Published by: Spiritual Quest
308 Tequesta Drive. Suite 20
Tequesta, Florida. 33469

Pho. (561) 754-2220
FAX (561) 754-2253

Cover Design by Jack Cuthrell

Graphics by Kurt Herring

TABLE OF CONTENTS

V

Acknowledgments

I've always been vaguely annoyed that actors and writers feel the need to publicly express their debt of gratitude. Besides, most people don't believe or read them.

Now I understand. Perhaps no other people spend the thousands of hours alone in their own thoughts, as writers and actors do. It is there we begin to realize how much we owe to others. Not just our loved ones, but every one that touches us. Good or bad.

I know I am what others have given me. My mother was a small, shy, self-effacing, tenacious lady. Yet, it was her unquestionable love that was and is, my support and strength. Her mark and signature is on me, and I am proud of it.

"Tim" my spiritual guide, knows me as no one else does, yet still stands beside me as a father; strong, tough and infinitely wise.

Dot, my sister, set a pace for me and I'm still trying to catch up. She taught me how to be ALIVE!!!

Barbara Harris Whitfield has been an inspiration ever since I saw her speaking in 1982. She is a beautiful, joyous light that has touched millions with her love and boundless enthusiasm.

It is my regret that I can not name each person who has contributed to my life. So to all of my friends and loved ones, I can only say thank you, and I love you.

When I was six, I awoke and found my
Great Grandmother standing beside my bed,
looking at me.

She had died two weeks earlier.

Great Grandmother had been born in 1841.
She still wore the styles of the 1870s:
full length, black, dresses; high collar, sleeves;
complete with black shoes, even in the summer.

Seeing her again after she died was nice and
without fear. After all, she was my Great
Grandmother.

We lived in Norfolk, Va. My parents drove to
Virginia Beach to see a medium named Edgar Cayce.
I can still remember his house. The foyer, the living
room and him. I remember his being a gentle man
with white hair. When the guests were seated, he
would lie on the couch and, within a few moments,
he would begin to speak. I was too young to
understand what he was saying, so I would sneak out
and play in the empty circle across the street.

At my age, the small mounted head of a deer that
was in the foyer was far more interesting than he
was. He of course became America's leading Psychic,
and millions have read his books.

My parents bought a house when I was eleven. After living there about six months, it came up in casual conversation that we had a ghost. After a few stories, the subject was dropped for lack of interest.

It came up again when our housekeeper said that she heard noises. She armed herself with a butcher's knife and went upstairs. The noise was coming from my mothers room. She threw open the door. No one was there, but the rocking chair was rocking fast, as though someone had just jumped out of it. It then slowed down to a stop. She check the room, the closets, under the bed, but no one was in the room.

Once she talked to us about the ghost, and found that all of us had heard it. She was not afraid, she just accepted it as "another ghost".

Mother, in talking to the former owner, was told that his son had died in the house. This was why he had sold their home.

Our "friend" stayed around for about two years. He was quiet and well behaved, a perfect house guest.

We would hear him moving around. We knew when he came into the room and when he left.

It was interesting, fun and normal. When we had other people to our home they would not hear him. Only our family heard him. Then when we stopped feeling his presence and hearing his sounds, we missed him. My Mother called the former owner and was told that he had just died. She concluded that the son had waited until his father died, then joined him.

It was during my enlistment in World War Two that I gave up believing in God. A God would not permit a War.

My next 40 years were full and interesting, but lacking in Spirituality. At fifty, I was divorced. I became a confirmed bachelor and an atheist. On a cool, clear, autumn day, a friend and I were going to my daughter's wedding. We had a picnic beside a lake, then walked through an oak forest in St. Cloud, Florida.

If you had seen us, you would have seen a couple walking, stopping for about five minutes, then resuming walking in silence. Not very impressive, but I walked away a totally different person.

For the next month, I was overwhelmed with curiosity. I had to know everything about God; the Bible, history, philosophy, religions, myths, everything about everything. I read and read and read.

A month later, my friend and I were waiting in an office with another couple. Just to pass the time, the owner brought out a Ouija board. Of course, he did not believe in them. It just happened to be in his office desk. The others tried it and it didn't work. No one expected it to work. It was just a silly game.

When my friend and I tried it, it moved fast! We had trouble keeping up with it. It turned out to be her Grandfather, dead for 40 years!

We were in shock! Talking to the dead! It was beyond our comprehension.

Just to talk it out, we went to an all night restaurant and spent hours over coffee trying to understand. We could not believe it! We had discovered the "TRUTH". Whatever that was.

The next morning, I bought my own board. Soon we gave that up. It was too slow. I tried "Automatic Writing" and gave that up. I then realized that I was hearing the words in my mind and writing them. I didn't need any help.

My friend became better at it than I was. While I was getting "Yes and No" answers, she was getting beautiful, complete letters from her Mother.

I asked if her Mother would write through me, and she agreed.

I could hear her in my mind very clearly, but all I received was "Love, Love". She filled a page with "Love, Love, Love, Love, Love, Love".

When I showed my friend, she began to cry. She told me for the first time that her Mother called her "Love"! Thus, her mother was telling me to "Love, Love", {to love her}! Which I did.

From then on it was one confirmation of proof after another. Situations that we could not know became known. The impossible became possible. At first, the voices that I "heard" were from people that I had known, before their deaths, with a few entities unknown to me. They were always intelligent, courteous, and as interested in me as I was in them. It was very much like meeting a stranger and having a nice talk. It was never anything frightening or unpleasant, ever.

The messages were complete, truthful, wise and beautiful. I would add the punctuation as needed, but I never changed a thought, by act or inference. I could not do that. Anything that I might add would only weaken their truths.

Over the past 18 years, I have received and saved some 14,000 hand written pages. I no longer keep count. Most are in answer to questions I have asked. From the beginning, they said that I would not be capable of understanding the answers until I was capable of asking the questions.

This is a gift that many authors, poets, musicians and artist have. Most do not mention it, or they refer to it as "inspiration" to explain it. I am totally convinced that everyone has it. Including you. If you would just quiet your mind, ask a question and listen for the answer. It will come, perhaps not the first time, but ultimately when you have quieted your mind enough, it will be there for you.

Do write it down, keep a note book. Take dictation, for I promise you, you will not remember it all. Like a dream, it fades with time. You will want to keep it's beauty and wisdom. It is for you.

They often gave me messages to deliver. That is a strange thing to have to do, to give a message from a person you do not know to a person you never met. I can not recall anyone doubting the message once they had read it.

I never pressed the point. They had the message. One lady cried when she read the letter. She knew that I could not have known the person, or what the message meant. She explained that the second paragraph was the prayer she and her husband said together, every evening.

My writing changed from personal questions to Spiritual Philosophy. They developed a profound truth, a perspective. There is a beauty that was way beyond my ability. They had a depth that I do not have, though I wish I did, but to say that would be a lie.

If you do not accept my story, then please read the letters for themselves, for their truths and beauty. The writing themselves say, "Our Proof is in our Truth".

These are my "Letters of the Soul"...

They were from Sweden and were in their Seventies. He was tall, strong and forthright. She was small, plump and laughing. They both loved each other very much. If you saw one, the other was there. If they were close, they were touching. If they spoke to each other, it was with endearments.

They had been childhood sweethearts and had married as soon as their parents gave their permission. They delighted in telling that they had been in love all of their lives.

Then late one night, she called to tell me that he had just died. Her voice was full of pain, helplessness.

I had nothing to give her except my clichés and platitudes. They were so inadequate, so empty. I had failed her.

Her pain was on my mind all night. The feeling that I had let her down haunted me. I was not there when she needed me.

At dawn, I asked for help from my inner voice and this message was given as a letter to her.

Grief from the passing of a loved one
is one of the greatest pains
that you can suffer.

It is in the pain that you realize
the value of the person.

Often, in the daily trials of life,
the person has been accepted
as just a part of your life.

Loved, yes, but in an ordinary way.
Someone who is there, sometimes pleasant,
sometimes annoying, to be counted on
and sometimes to be disappointed by.

In the pain of their absence,
you feel the full power of their value to you.
How much they comforted you.
How much they cared and loved you
and how empty your life is without them.

The degree of your pain should not be looked
upon as punishment that God has inflicted,
but rather a mirror held for you to see
the depth of their love and your love
for each other.

A realization of the love that was not fully appreciated
until the absence was felt.

Do know that they have not left you,
they are not lost,
nor are they gone from your life.
They are with you and share your life
now, perhaps more than ever.
Every time you think of them,
remember them, feel their presence.
They are with you and share your emotions.

Do not grieve for them, for they are free of the problems of life.
Allow yourself to grieve for you, for you are the one that has been
temporarily left behind.

Allow yourself to feel all
the emotions that you have.
Until you feel the full range of your grief,
you can not be free of it.

They share your feelings,
and know that your pain, anger and
feeling of abandonment are but the colors
that paint the full picture of your love for them,
and they love you for it.

There were many days when they were alive,
but not in your presence, that they comforted you and
supported you just by your knowing that they were there.
If they were not there, at that moment, you knew they
would be back and that was comforting.

Know, with all of your heart, that they are not dead, just
their body.

That they are alive, happy and healthy,
more than they could be when they were in their body.

That their purest and highest qualities
have been enhanced with their passing.

That their lesser qualities,
caused by the problems of life and body,
have ceased to be.

If they loved you, while with you,
they love you more now.
For they see with a greater perspective
and wisdom, your values.

That they wait for you
to live out your full range
of life normally,
so that you will join them
in the happiness
called Heaven.

Whenever I speak of Life, the subject of Death arises. Our society treats death as the ultimate loss. The one thing to avoid at all cost. The one last insult and failure. Our greatest fear.

So when I asked for understanding of death, this was the unexpected answer.

Death is the freer of the soul.
I know that when living
it is difficult to understand.

When the soul is released from the body
it rejoices, free from pain,
free from fear,
free from the aging, or sick body.

Like a beautiful dove
released from the cage.
Free to return to the sky,
which was, is
and always will be
it's home.

To be Humble...

Humbleness is not saying,
"I am not worthy."

It is saying, "Thank you, for your love and concern."

It is acknowledging the other person
as being worthy.

It is not asking for love and appreciation,
but rather giving it.

The opposite of humbleness is arrogance.
Arrogance is an expression of contempt
and contempt is the opposite of love.

Humbleness is turning the spotlight of attention from
yourself, toward the other person.

Humbleness is not saying "I am bad",
but rather, "You are good".

At a time when some women feel they have the right to protect their own lives and bodies, other equally good women feel that abortions are murder and sinful. I asked about abortions.

Abortion is a grave responsibility that does not give itself to easy answers and is never always right or always wrong.

The fetus does not become a living being until it is separated from its mother. Until the time occurs it can be said to be a part of the mother's body, an organ, that is growing within the mother, a spiritual possibility.

It is only when the infant has been separated from the mother, by whatever means, does the spirit enter and life begins. To kill the baby then is the killing of a life, thus to be avoided at all cost.

The true problem of abortion
is the decision made to conceive,
or the decision to place one's self
in the situation to conceive.

Sex is a beautiful, joyous thing,
but it carries responsibility.
If you are not prepared to face the birth
of a child, you should not risk it's happening.

Granted there are times when it is unavoidable, then, to
remove the sperm or abort as soon as possible which should
carry no guilt, and is justified.

To use abortion as a form of birth control
is to risk your own life, as well as to assure a guilt that may
last a life time.

That guilt affects not only you,
but others that you hold dear
and will color your life and their lives
far beyond the value gained.

When I was young it seemed that every man and woman was married. That being with someone was simply a fact of life. Over my life time I have seen that change. Now, most people still want to marry but do not. They are afraid to commit, or they are married and wish they were not. Some are divorced, but were and are now, still lonely. It seems that loneliness is an epidemic.

So I asked the question. What is the cause of so much loneliness?

Loneliness is the failure of the heart
to obtain the true love it seeks.
It is an emptiness created when the heart
does not find the one person
that can fill that need.

Yet, life offers many people
who are capable of love.

In the course of one's life
people enter, share, and leave
as a river flows.
It is almost unending,
regardless of time, place and age.

So why does the heart not find
the one true love?
It is in the expectations
that the problem lies.
The creation of expectations
that are beyond the possible.
A looking for each and every detail
to be met by the other,
rather than opening of the heart to receive.

A seeing of beauty that is,
rather than what should be.
A giving of Love
that creates Love,
rather than asking for Love.

I had asked about my inability to express my thoughts clearly. When I reread this I saw for the first time the joke that was embedded within it and exploded with laughter. Which I would not have done if "I" had written it.

Your language does not have the ability to express thoughts of life and God. So everything becomes an attempt to create words that can explain, and thus, misleads in the effort.

Your mind can know thoughts your tongue cannot express.

Look how mathematicians express their knowing in letters and numbers. The facts exist even if the numbers are not there.

So the thought starts out on the wrong foot, but of course, there is no foot.

This thought on trust so true and profound, I wish, somehow that it could be a part of every love vow for every couple.

Trust is necessary before you can love,
and love is necessary for life.

To give your love and thus life to a person,
you must trust them.

If you are to give your love, your emotions,
your life to them, there must be a quality in
them that says,

"I will not betray you, what you give me I will
protect. That for your trust I will trust".

Trust is a form of faith, a form of expectation.

One can not truly love another

if they are afraid of them. How can you give,

if in giving, your are hurt?

Yes, there will be times in giving of doubt.

Two people cannot be in complete agreement

on everything at all times. It cannot be.

Those are the times

that you give your trust,

not withdraw it.

For there cannot be perfect cooperation

without one becoming a slave of the other.

It is in times of conflict

that it is necessary to trust the most.

When you trust, you are saying, "I love you,
I know you are trustworthy,
even though we may disagree.
I know that your intentions
are of the highest and I agree with you
even though I may not agree with every decision
and opinion that you may have".

With two people, loving and trusting each other,
the conflicts are not a matter of principle,
but rather a matter of implementing of life.

When I began this book, I spoke of the "Voice", in the abstract use of the word. But you can't communicate with a voice, learn to trust it, respect it, love it and still call it and think of it as a "Voice".

I asked if (it) had a name. The voice said: "*Yes, my name is Tim*".

I said, "do you want me call you Timothy"?

Tim, answered, "*No, I'll earn my own respect, thank you*".

From that moment on I had a friend, a Teacher, a Patriarch that was available to me anytime, anyplace. All I needed was to quiet my mind, ask a question and Tim was there for me.

Other than one time, when I misunderstood his message, have I ever had reason to doubt him.

At that time, when I told him that I did not accept this message, he responded by saying, *"Good! Don't trust me. Make me prove myself to you. Weigh everything I say on the scale of your own wisdom and your own truth. I will never command you on anything. All I can do is offer my advice and you must make the decision and take the responsibility for the results. I can not"*.

After 19 years and counting, I can honestly say that never has his advice been wrong or has mislead me, never. I can also say that there have been times that I did not do what he had suggested and wished I had. I must be a slow learner.

I said, "If there is a God, there must be a Heaven".

Man has always thought that Heaven
was up there in the sky.
He looks to the sky and the clouds
as the destination of man's soul.

Yet, Heaven is a very real place, but it is
real in the sense of man's reaction to it.

For the soul that is energy
Heaven does exist, but Heaven
is the creation of man's soul.

Heaven is a place of rest,
a place to reflect,
to meditate in all the fullness
that the soul can bear.

It is not in one place,
but being thought
is wherever the energy is.

It is the manifestation of all
that man can conceive of
in beauty, peace, love.

The soul can create it's own
or share another's Heaven,
or the total manifestation.

When the soul has had it's fill
of the visual Heaven
it becomes more interested in God.

The soul no longer needs to receive
it's pleasures from the visual
when it has not physical eyes,
or needs a place to live
when it does live without the body.

So, as the physical trappings of the body
fade away, (as eating is no longer needed
when you are not hungry) the conscious,
that is the true you, is free
of the body's remembered longings.

Then it can be free.

Free to enjoy and know God.

To understand His beauty and strength,

to be a part of Him,

to be one with Him, to share in what

and who He is, to submerge the self

into the One of God.

It is here that the soul's

energy is refilled, nourished.

When that is done the soul awakens

to the concept of returning to the body,

to work again on earth,

to bring the love and wisdom of God to earth, to help

mankind grow and prosper toward God,

to lift mankind out of it's self inflected hell.

From the very beginning the letters spoke of LOVE.
It seemed that in any and every subject matter
somehow, some way, the word LOVE was used in
the answer.

I really did not understand the attention to LOVE.
Of course, I realize now, that the problem was mine.
Our society use of the word LOVE is almost limited
to romantic love or speaking of family love, or puppy
love, and so did I.

LOVE, used as the letters spoke of is far more,
much more, than simple every day love. I will not try
to explain. The writings are eloquent enough.

The lesson today is one of love.
It is always love
because love is the energy of the Universe.

Love is the life that was breathed
into every living thing.
A love that allows each thing
to reach out for its own existence.

A Love that allows everything to become its own creator.

A love that gives and asks only to be loved in return.

I know it is hard to understand,
for your use of the word does not allow that.
But understand that love is more,
far more, than just a pleasant emotion.

It is a force, an energy, power,
a presence of life and power.
It is love that is the power of creation.

All of creation is a product of Love.
For love in this case refers to
the creative thought,
a thought of growth,
a thought that foresaw
what it was creating
and became its own thought.

A thought that is so great,

so vast, so overwhelming

that even in its existence

man can not comprehend it.

Love is the strength that is given to all

to protect themselves and their loved ones.

Is there anything braver than the parent

defending its own.

It is the strength that propels men

to work for a life time, to give to their

loved ones the care and food necessary

so that they may repeat the cycle

with the next generation.

Is not love expressed in everything

that is beautiful,

every flower,

every change of season,

every sunrise and sunset,

and every new born baby?

In any talk of Hell, the Devil, and Demons it seems
that the purpose is to raise fear and with fear there
can be control. My question. What of hell, the devil,
and demons? Tim's answer was....

*Demons are not a reality, but are rather
man's projecting his beliefs on himself.*

*Seeing the evil he has done he wishes to
punish himself and does so by creating the
demons to do the work. But, this is man's
work.... God loves, not punishes.*

*Each soul reviews his life and sees the harm
done, the opportunity not seized, the love not
given and though it is painful it is a pain of the
heart rather than the body which is no more.*

*The creation of demons is by men who do
not have the wisdom to see that they are
the creators.*

SEX AND LUST

Ah, Sex. The most thought of, talked about, denied, boasted, condemned and praised of all subjects. Why should I be the exception, so I asked, and got this interesting and thoughtful answer.

Sexuality is the means that one generation creates the next. In one form or another it is found in every living thing.

Other than in the lowest of cells, sex is the only means of procreation. As such, it is of great importance. It is a part of every male and female and the future of all depends upon it.

God presents it as the greatest pleasure. For this we are willing to go anywhere, do anything to fulfill this need and experience the joy of physical love.

You can see it in all species, without exceptions.

Though, what you cannot understand, is the other specie's

pleasure, for it looks so different from yours.

Yet know, that it is there

no matter how remote in appearance

it is from yours.

It is from sex that all other pleasures grow,

the home, the babies, the love, the closeness,

the security are hinged on this need fulfilled.

Lust is a distortion of this emotion.

A seeking for the pleasure of sex

without assuming the responsibility

of the home and family.

LUST cont.

Using the other person without regard
to their needs and wants.
It is a focusing on the act only
without the accompanying emotion and love.

Like all sins,
it is not the act itself that is wrong,
but the excesses of it, that becomes the sin.
Food is necessary for life,
yet, overindulgence can ruin your life.
Working is necessary to survive,
but for those that do it for itself alone
waste the purpose for doing it.

Sex and lust are the same.
With sex being a beautiful and
necessary part of life
and lust being a distortion of it
that can lead to despair and loneliness.

Sex has its fulfillment.
Lust has its emptiness.

When this voice started trying to teach me I was a very devout, conscience, atheist. A good man, kind, but the idea of a God sitting on a throne, threatening me with hell and damnation if I did not Love Him just didn't cut it with me.

Each denomination claiming to be the Pathway to the "ONE TRUE GOD" didn't do the cause of God any good either. He was God for everyone or he wasn't a God.

It was far more acceptable to believe in evolution and cause and effect. So all of this talk of God left me cold.

How could it be I was polite and let this talk of God go unnoticed for a while, then I begin to listen....

This ocean of oneness that is God
exceeds any and all understanding.
But it does exist and has always existed
and always will exist
and grows larger, richer and more
profound with each passing day.

*Just as you can look down to the atoms and
molecules and lookup to the universe
and see the same energy and shapes.
Then know that it is without limit or end
in either direction.*

*Loving God should be a part
of every man's life.
There are other things to be done too.
Man must learn how to translate GOD's message
into life, to bring it down to the practical use.*

*For what good is love
if no one is loved?
What good is peace
if it does not stop war?*

*Yes, to make an effort to love God
and demonstrate it
should be in the application of the love.*

There is so much need in the world,
to prove that love,
by feeding the poor,
caring for the sick, young and old
is the proper demonstration
of your love of God.

Try to find God in everything.
See the greater purpose in everything.
Know that God and life are inseparable.
What is, is God.

See man's weakness, meanness,
as just a way for that man to find God.
Yes, he is weak and he is mean,
but that does not mean
he is unworthy of your love and respect.

There is stupidity and greed
and there should not be.
It is wrong, but to condemn it, hurts you.
Within everything is possibility of growth.
Your eyes should focus on that, not the error.

Use your power to correct what is wrong,
rather than condemn it.

See in each person,
a God that is trying
to escape that place that it is.
Like a bird trying to escape the cage.
Love the man, not his condition
even if he created it,
for he did not mean
to create the final condition.

It is in finding God in everything
that you become more of a tool of GOD's Love.
It is in taking away your darkness
that you become more of a Light.

And God knows the world needs more Light.
Be one of them.

Give and you receive.

Love and you are loved.

Enjoy and you are enjoyed.

These are the basic components of life.

It is so simple, so obvious, so logical.

So why is it so hard to understand

when each person benefits from it.

It is not a giving up,

a self sacrifice,

a heavy and painful task.

It is a joy,

a pleasure,

a happiness,

a fulfillment,

a reward,

and it is yours

for the giving.

ACCEPTANCE

In reading books and articles about mental health and relationships I came across the word "acceptance" over and over again.

Of course, I knew the definition of the word but there seemed to be a meaning beyond that. When something bothers me I have to seek the answer. The dictionary told me exactly what I had thought. My other searches did not give me the answer. I wanted to know.

Here was an interesting situation, I did not know something. Yet, I am going to ask my "Tim", or if you wish, my inner self, for an answer I knew I did not know.

I asked Tim. Immediately, without a seconds delay, he began answering and telling me that which I did not know. He filled a whole page, going far beyond what I had thought would be possible. He told me without stopping, or thinking the subject over, or digressing, something I could not have done.

The answer is beautiful, profound and beyond my abilities. This became one of my proofs that these messages come from another source, other and greater than I am.

Acceptance is the act of being able to have
your life and enjoy it
without having to approve of it.

It is not necessary that you are always in
control.
You do not have to have it your way.
You do not have to enjoy your life
to live a rich and rewarding life.

Life has many facets.
There is so much to learn
from each and every moment,
that to say you must approve of it,
is to limit your growth
to that which you know and entertains you.

ACCEPTANCE cont.

When you can accept life in all of it moods, then you
become an audience to yourself. No longer trying to write
the script, but giving yourself to the play.

Learning and growing from what unfolds,
seeing life as an adventure,
having change, both good and bad,
with every turn in the trail.
Seeking the feelings, the emotions,
as lessons to learn.

When you can accept life and still live contentedly, then
you have taken away life's ability to damage you. For you
see each happening as an experience to feel, know and learn
from a step in your path
to knowing God.

My writing of this is one week after the Oklahoma City bombing. A disaster that we all must share, at least, a small part of the blame. That we have created a society that this could even be conceived of, much less carried to completion, is a horror. Even worse, we have people on TV justifying this obscenity.

This letter of the soul is appropriate now more than ever. Yet, Tim wrote it over six years ago.

I want you to realize that nothing
in the world existed before the thought.
Not the world, the ocean, or the sky.
It first had its origin in the mind of God.

Just as all buildings, roads and war
have their origins in the mind of man.

The world that you know is of man.
God gave you the universe
and you men turned your area of it
into a hole that you wish to escape, back to
the world before man, peace, forest, nature.

Man sees the problem and seeks to escape it,
though the only answer is to change
the mind of man, so that the plans of man lead
to a world of love and peace.

Cities can be made that please the mind of man.
Homes can be built that allow
the beauties of nature in.

Families can return to being the fountainhead
of love, peace and security.
Man must learn that he is the master of his own fate.
That he cannot blame God
for what he has done.

Let man take the responsibility for his actions, knowing
that he must make a world of peace or die in a war of his
own making.

The answer, as always, lies in Love.
God has given you the stage for your play,
but the script is yours.

He watches the play and longs
for your happy ending,
but the final act is not over.

Give the play a happy ending
with all men living, learning,
growing and loving.
Otherwise, the whole history of man is lost
and your life and the life of your family,
lost along with the rest.

Please try to do your share
to change the play.

It is of all importance.

LUCIFER

This morning I read in the Bible a description of a military battle being fought by Lucifer and the Archangel Michael. In this battle each man fought each day, and won or lost each day. So how could this be?

While driving on a busy highway I thought of asking Tim. Tim's voice spoke within my head, "Why wait? I am here now." So this was his answer, while I drove in traffic.

The battles of Lucifer and Michael
are fought every day, in every person,
for the pull of evil and the need to be
virtuous is a battle that each person fights.

The battle never ends, for in each of us is
the desire to be evil, yet the need to be good,
by each of us, each day, and it is won one
person at a time. When all people win,
(are good) the Devil will die.

Peace is the most desired human condition and the
most rare. This is Tim's response.

Now, let us imagine a world without war.

*Roads that lead everywhere with no
boundaries, cities that bring together all
that is best in all people, an open flow of
knowledge on all subjects, available to all
people.*

*Children being born, in love
and assuming adulthood, in love.*

*This is yours. It is in your reach.
You have the power. It all comes to just a
matter of collective desire.*

*When enough people see this goal,
know of its possibility,
and refuse to be a part of anything else.*

WAR cont.

No man can gain power without the cooperation of others.

Tyrants must work though others.

He must, in the beginning,

work through persuasion,

through voluntary cooperation of others,

to gain power.

Think for a moment of all the horrors

and all the waste, and all of the lives lost by war.

What have we bought by this carnage?

There is nothing that has been gained,

that could not have been gained through

peaceful means.

Usually, it has been only the fulfillment

of one man's dreams, if he won.

Others have been carried along in his dream.
In every case power, domination and wealth
was the reward expected.

Thousands, millions killed,
generations destroyed.
The creation of endless lives of labor,
ground under foot, and for what purpose?

So that one man could stand victorious over millions.

Yes, some wars have been fought against a tyrant, and it
was perhaps necessary to defend your nation and lives,
but the original source of the war was one man's hunger
for dominance.

Some magnificent cities have been built
by plundering whole nations,
and turning their people into slaves.

Did war itself create the talent, the art?
No, it was already there,
with or without the war.

People, many people, must surrender their will to him,
and accept his goals, as their goals, for him to succeed.
When people refuse to give him
this needed strength,
then he will be powerless, impotent.
When the people can see that,
their best interest and their children's
best interest and thus the world's best interest lies in peace.
Then you can build your paradise.

This will be brought into reality,
when you make your choice,
and exercise your free will.

Living alone, I gained 40 lbs., then lost 70. Ending
up being unable to stay awake, a walking skeleton.
The doctors were unable to find anything wrong. At
the end, I lay in bed with a note pinned to my pillow,
telling whoever found me to notify my adult
children.

Then a friend that I had not heard from for the past
seven years showed up at my door, bags in hand. He
moved in uninvited, but very welcome. He started
feeding me, caring for me. In a week, we were
arguing politics, fighting over what TV show to
watch, having fun, talking and bantering,
and I got well!

My friend's presence had healed me.

My doctors later told me that it was not their care
that had healed me, and that it helped keep them
humble.

I now surround myself with family and friends
and my health is perfect. My heart power has
doubled, I'm having a wonderful life. Thus, I
introduce Tim's letter.

Your soul's health

Your bodies health is in direct response
to your soul's health.
What your soul creates, your body suffers.

Live your life in love and beauty
and your soul is healthy.
Live your life in darkness
and your body suffers.

Now, this should not be taken as an absolute,
for your body also, must suffer
the illness of the society's soul.
You live in a society
that can inflict itself on others.

What one generation does
can affect the next generation.
What one person does to the environment
can, and does, affect others.
One evil person can change many lives.

If it were possible to separate one soul from other souls,
then the body would be in direct response to the soul's
health.
This is not to be taken as a esoteric reaction, but a direct
action.
Does not the good person treat his body with love.
Providing for whatever
it needs: good food, clean water, fresh air, cleanliness,
exercise, and rest.

Does not the neglectful person
abuse his body with excesses:
drinking, overeating, physical pleasures,
beyond the bodies capacity?

When we say that illness is the lack of love, it is not to
imply that every ill person is neglectful, for the person can
well be the victim of someone else's lack of love.

So the blame is not on the ill person, rather in the illness
that had it's source, in the lack of love.

GOD's love and energy
flows through the universe
at all times.
It is the power of Life.

When a person is ill,
it can be said that
the person is closed off
from the energy source.
That some emotion, or thought
has deprived the body
of its ability
to resist the illness or pain.

When a person heals,
they are giving their love and energy
and if you have that energy,
it came from God.

His energy is flowing through you
to the ill person,
replenishing their lack.

A Love that allows everything to become its own creator.

A love that gives and asks
only to be loved in return.

I know it is hard to understand,
for your use of the word does not allow that.
But understand that love is more,
far more, than just a pleasant emotions.

It is a force, an energy,
a presence of life and power.
It is love that is the power of creation.

All of creation is a product of Love.
For love in this case refers to
the creative thought,
a thought of growth,
a thought that foresaw what it was creating
and become its own thought.

Love and you are loved.
Give your love freely,
help others, protect the weak,
assist the needful.

Project what you want for yourself,
focus on beauty, health and happiness
and you will have them.

Yes, you can change the world.
It was made bad and ugly
by those that did not care or love.
So care and love.

They made the difference over the years.
Now you can make a difference.
You have the future!

Save your world!
No one else will,
except those who care and love.
Join with them and defend your life
and our future.

Your thoughts create your world.
What you think and believe
becomes your world.

You and you alone control your mind,
thus your thoughts.

You are in a world that includes everything.
Beauty, ugliness, love, anger,
Gratitude, rejection, joy, pain,
everything there is has an opposite.

It is your choice, what you see
and what you believe.

Focus your mind on beauty and joy
and you will find it.
Look for anger and pain,
it is there, waiting.

You think it and you create it.
Your thoughts become your world.
It is your choice.

The Poor and Homeless...

It is not God's will that they are without food
and God does try to answer their request,
but he is not always able to help.
Thus there are more things to be considered
than just their wanting and needing for
God's Love to work.

God can and does help if there are the means to help,
but often man creates a world that prevents God from
working.
Men must learn to live together
so that their conditions do not prevent God from helping.

Man's free will, also meaning
man and his society,
have to take the responsibility
for their actions and thoughts.

Being grateful is a step up in your growth.

When you can see the help others have given you,

you can begin giving help to others

without the feeling of pride or vanity.

When you are able to help others

you are not being good or virtuous,

but rather you are paying off a debt

of help and support that others have given you.

So, you should do it with a feeling of gratitude.

Charity is not an act of virtue or prideful giving,

but rather an opportunity to share your good fortune

that was given to you,

by others.

During the untold hours I have spent listening to this gentle voice, I moved from being an atheist to the number one fan of God. He is my best friend, my Father. I have asked questions about Him over and over again. Each time the answer is given. Totally consistent and yet totally a new perspective, a different view. This is just one of them.

He is beyond comprehension, now and forever.
Though you may eventually become a part of Him
you will never be able to grasp the all of Him.

He does exist and your life is your proof.
Nothing that man has done or will ever do
will equal the creation of life.

Life has its many forms, sizes, complexity.

*Know that all life, matter, and energy of the universe is
but a part of God. That vastness is as concerned about you
as your own mother would be
and His love is as tender and as personal as a child's
emotion.
His love is an ever present force to enjoy
as is the air you breath.*

*His only desire
is that you live your life in love
and health and happiness,
while knowing
that the problems and illness and pain of life are
but temporary lessons
that you must learn,
in order to strengthen yourself
for your return to Him.*

*God awaits you,
to share Himself
with you.*

MY MARRIAGE

Marriage used to be for a "lifetime of wedded bliss". Everyone that went down the aisle, took a vow "for better or worse, in sickness and in health, until death do us part". Now, half of all marriages fail, leaving millions of "latch key" single parent children. Why?

We all marry with the greatest of hopes and desires and expectations. Marriage is instinctual. We need each other. Every fiber of our bodies and every thought and dream calls out to be with the person we love. Yet we fail. Why?

Good people with the best of intention and effort can not get along with the person they loved and choose to marry. Why?

Perhaps that is too kind. It too often becomes a matter of hate, loathing, contempt.

Then a willingness to do anything, pay anything to be free of the person we loved. Why?

I do not write on marriage from the point of view of someone that succeeded and had a wonderful marriage, or someone that has never married. No, I am a two time loser. I know the pain and disappointment of having marriages fail.

I know the hurt and sense of failure caused to the other one, the one I loved. I know the loneliness and disruption caused to children, how it affected their lives. I know what it is to start over again at the age of 47 and again at 64.

With this background, I asked Tim the "Why?" I have been asking you. This was his profoundly beautiful answer. I can only wish I had this advice before and during the marriages. This is the information that should be taught, not only in school, but before any marriage. It is inspired.

If you are married, or about to be, read this, study it, take it into your soul and make it a part of your life.

Later, in reading other Spiritual books I have found
the same thoughts expressed over and over again in
different words.

Please read these letters aloud and slowly,
preferably to your partner, alone if necessary. Even if
you are unmarried or alone, read them and believe
them.

When you are unhappy with your marriage
all things are affected. The way you see
things, the work you do, the thoughts you think,
all are reactions to
the happiness or unhappiness
in your marriage.

When you love your wife, you love life.
When you are angry at her,
you are angry at life.

Love takes on a far greater
importance than just your love
for one person.

It is a great motivater.
It reaches into every aspect of your life.

Allow the person you love to be free.
Allow her to live her life, fulfill her needs
and reach out and grow herself.
Then love her for doing so.

Do not think that you have any right to her,
that she owes you anything.
Love what she is
not what you would make of her.

Allow her love to be given
to you freely,
as a gift.

Both of you want love,
but both of you want it on your terms.

Both have preconceived ideas and dreams of marriage that are not fulfilled by the other and that does not make either of you wrong or bad.

As each person grows up they look forward to a dream of what marriage is going to be and it is seldom.

Your expectations are unreal and the person you marry is real and it is in the difference, that the pain begins.

Each of you try hard to fulfill your role in that dream and expect the other to respond to your expectations.
They can't.

Each of you are working from a script
but each has different scripts,
thus your thoughts and words don't
rhyme or make sense.

A woman cannot be a dream wife
and the man cannot be a dream husband.

Now, what do you do?

You can live your life in an armed camp,
each ready to lash out at the other
whenever the words are not right.

Or you can separate.
Will that bring happiness to either?
I think not.

Or you can accept the other as they are.
Not demanding changes that are impossible,
Nor giving up your life to please the other.

Simply say,
"You are my spouse
and I love you
and I accept you as you are.

I will stand here and you stand there.
I will love you without trying to control you
and I hope you can love me,
without trying to control me.

I accept you for the qualities that you have
and love you for them without allowing
those qualities that intrude upon my life,
to hurt me.

I give you the right to live your life
while sharing my life
and I ask that you do the same,
all in the name of
love".

As in perhaps, no other situation,
is love more important.

In fact, without love there is no reason
for the relationship to exist,
for it is created out of love, for love
and without love it is filled with pain,
distrust, loneliness.

Each person is born with the need to give
and receive love from another person.
It is a need that can at times,
supersede almost all other desires and needs.

Each person lives their life in anticipation
searching, desiring love.

When it is found,
it is the fulfillment of all of life's desires.

This is the person,
that will give you happiness forever!
Your life has now begun!

This person gives your life meaning and purpose
beyond your wildest dreams!

The other person, your loved one,
is experiencing the same emotions and needs.

But alas, each of you are real people
with faults, weakness, strengths, courage and fears.

Each of you have lived different lives,
have different needs, different expectations.

It is in these differences
that the problems begin.
Neither of you are wrong or bad.
You are just different
and romantic love expects perfection.

There is no one
that can meet your dreams.
No one! Does this mean the end of love?

Not at all, for it is in the differences
that each person learns the real meaning of love.
Not a love born of fantasy,
but a love born of giving and taking.
A sharing of self, a blending of minds,
thoughts, bodies.

A love shaped by compassion, friction,
doubt and faith and always, love.

The dream of love in all reality cannot exist,
but because of it we go into marriage
and find a love that is so much deeper
that it can endure illness, disappointment,
old age and even death.

The learning process of marriage
is difficult and painful.
There are things you must give,
dreams that must be changed,
expectations that will never be met.

If these changes are not made,
then the marriage will fail
and you are left with the even greater
pain of guilt, remorse, loneliness
and failure.

When we love a person
we want them to fit our needs.
They are the one who must fulfill our needs.
They can't anymore than you can fulfill theirs.

So what can you do?

Stand on your own two feet and live your life
to the best of your ability.
Accomplish what you want,
be who you want to be
and allow them to do likewise.

Do not make your marriage your life.
Make it your home, your refuge, your reward.

When each of you are living
your life to its fullest
then the compromises of marriage
assume a far lesser role.

The problems of health, money, arguments
are the problems of both
to be worked through jointly.

It then becomes not two people against each other
but rather two people standing together
against the world.

The purpose of marriage is love.
The two words should have the same name
because with love a marriage exists,
without love it does not.

It is in love that the joy of marriage grows.

This should be kept foremost in your mind.
Every act in marriage should be
sweetened with love.

Oh, I know how hard that can be,
but who said it would be easy?

It is a life time commitment
of all of your gentlest loving,
most compassionate emotions
to one person.

In fact, your choices are love or anger.
Which serves you best?

You can have the momentary pleasure
of hurting, but what does it gain you?

No, it only hurts the other person
and then they must have their revenge,
more hurt and a failing marriage.

When fatigue, problems, rejection enters,
this becomes extremely difficult.
You want to lash out to hurt, to place blame,
but this is the very time to give
love and reassurance.

You can hold your tongue and realize the other person is suffering and disappointed, or they would not be angry. Accept their rage and give them love and support. Reassure them of your steadfast love.

This is by far the more difficult of the two choices. Though it does not guarantee happiness, the anger does guarantee unhappiness.

Love in marriage is not expressed in raging passion unending, but in the quietness of acceptance.

The having of a companion that is always there for you despite the problems of the day, knowing you, loving you.

Jokingly I have said that I went through World War Two, never got hurt, never hurt anyone else, and never even got mad. To some degree that is true. Even a Dentist said that I am so calm that I am certifiably dead.

But let me get angry at my wife and it is the end of the Earth!! "It is all over! finished! done with!". Though I don't say those things, it is what I am thinking. This is because there is so much pain and a feeling of betrayal that cuts too deeply.

So this Letter was from Tim to me following an argument with my wife. About what? I don't even remember.

Anger in marriage is a fact of life.
Marriage cannot truly fulfill itself
if anger is not expressed.

Continued...

Anger comes into marriage
as a summer thunderstorm.
It consumes itself quickly
and the skies clear
and everything is peace and quietness again
and the world is richer for the experience.

Or it can be said that anger is like housecleaning,
a necessary and unpleasant chore,
but needed to keep your home clean and happy.
Well worth the effort.

Anger is a real but temporary emotion
caused by the friction of two normal people
living together in marriage.

All cannot be perfect.

Desires, ambitions, needs,
habits are always different.

Anger erupts when one person
doing the right thing
offends the other
who is doing the right thing
and no harm is intended.

The need to react
and correct the differences
is strong and needs to be shown.

It is in the expressing of that hurt
in anger, that if received
with love and patience,
merely helps to polish the marriage
until it shines again
with love and forgiveness,
as old wood shines with
an ever deepening depth
with the passage of time
and polishings.

The dolphins are God's life
brought to it's happiest.
Their minds are bright and full of life.
Man could learn from them.
They do not kill the world they live in
and they do follow God's law.

They do not need to build cities.
They are complete in themselves.

They have a soul though not in the same way as you.
That is not to say a lower soul,
just different.

Man may be brighter in the ways of the world,
but the dolphins are so far ahead of you in love,
companionship and understanding.
Man could only be made richer by copying them.

The dolphins have solved all of their problems of life and
now just lives enjoying his life and loves.
How complete can you be?

FEAR

Fear is your reaction to the unknown.
When you remove the ignorance
you remove the fear.

Having faith and trust in God
is the surest way to avoid fear.
Trust God to love you and
His loving you will lead you
through most of the fears in life.

Think for a moment of your life.
You have had fears and doubts and worries
almost every day.
Have these fears been justified?
Haven't most of your fears
dissolved before they occurred?
Did you find a way to solve the problem,
to face it head on or side step it?
Can you even remember what you were afraid last year
or 10 years ago?
Put your faith in God's help
and most of your fear will never be realized.

Writing for Tim has changed my life. I was an atheist, now I'm a believer. Sailing the islands was my greatest ambition. Now I have a wonderful life teaching Tim's lessons to groups in churches and on the radio. Giving Tim's truths to anyone that may need them and helping them!

But it is interesting how I am perceived. It has been strongly, politely, quietly, suggested by some that I am ill and drugs and hospitals can help me. Others at the top of their voices say that I am "infested with demons". (Isn't that a wonderful turn of words, what a mental picture it suggested).

Fortunately, the vast majority accept what I teach. They may not understand the source, but acknowledge the truths.

So in this next letter Tim explains what he is and what he does and how this communication is just a part of God's Love.

Cont ...

Tim cont.

We of the Spirit World see and watch over the people we love. We follow your lives, watching your successes and losses, feeling the joy and the pain you have, knowing your strengths and weakness.

As is perfectly normal we wish to help, to offer advice and council to our loved ones just as a loving parent wishes to aid their child.

Our thoughts and feelings are often felt by the living. They sense our presence and our energy. You know when another person comes into a room or another person has strong emotions about you.

cont...

Tim cont.

This is not different from what we feel or do. In fact, it is the same.

Some people are so involved in their own thoughts they sense nothing else. There are those that do not listen to someone who is talking directly to them. They are so tied to their own point of view, their own self-centeredness.

While other's who are more quiet and serene, can feel and know us.

Once you begin to take the time to become quiet, to leave your mind open to feelings and thoughts other than your own,
our thoughts and words are heard.

Tim cont.

The life force, the power and energy of life
that is within your body is the person you are.
That life force does not cease
with the death of your body.
It never ceases.

Thus we are no different from you,
except at this time
you are in the physical form
and we are not,
though we are every bit as alive.

Our contact and our communication with you
is just as normal as your communication
with any person, except lacking a physical
tongue and a physical body to carry it.
Our communication is of thought and emotion.

The stronger the emotion
the more energy the emotion has and
the stronger and clearer our thoughts.
The more conscientious your listening,
the more able we are to be heard.

We work through your mind and your language
and your five senses. If we are giving you
our thoughts and you are listening,
then the communication can be completed.

You have the power to accept or reject
our thoughts. We must have your acceptance,
before this can be completed. Whether or not you
consciously think of it. We cannot intrude into your
thoughts, except when you allow us or there is such
extreme emotion, such as physical danger,
as to be heard by you.

Since we cannot benefit or profit from our contact with you, our motivation is only one of love and concern.

Again, very much the parent
to child relationship.
The parent wishes the child to grow and live his life fully and richly.
Thus we watch our loved ones
and only wish to aid and advise them
so to increase their happiness and well-being.

Each of us teach that love is all.
This love is the force of the universe
and that the answer to all of man's
problems is Love.

It is difficult to keep writing that,
for the words do not do justice to the thought.

cont.

The language of the tongue
fails to convey all the thoughts
that we must share.

Thus the silent language of mediation
comes into play.
For it is in meditation that you find silence
and within that silence,
is the sharing of thoughts
that transcends words.

Your ears do not hear,
but your heart does
and you learn
from within.

ALIENS-UFO

Abductions, Aliens, UFO sighting are becoming a part of our culture. Myself, I know nothing of them, but I have friends that have seen them. They are honorable, trust worthy and I believe them. So I asked Tim for his answer.

Just think of how different the many Gods are,
how different the many miracles have been,
how different the religious artifacts are.

All express God, all are different,
not because God is, but because man is.

Now the UFOs are to reach man
of the technical world.
Man values science,
so we give him an object of mystery
to study and hopefully in studying it,
he will find and understand God.

Give man a chance to drop his chain of ignorance
and man will soar.
Man limits himself to what has been proven
and questions the unproven
and in questioning, grows.

We will always be one step ahead of man,
thus leading him by his own inquisitiveness.

No, UFOs are not real.
Yes, UFOs are real to those who seek.

All twelve step programs and most Spiritual teachings regardless of the origin recommend "surrendering" your life to a higher being.

Now that is hard to do! Everything we learn in our life tells us to take control of our lives. That we and we alone should make our own decisions. That we must make our life what we want it to be. That we are the boss!

Yet in the course of life we sometimes lose control. We become lost. Everything is going wrong. We need help. We need advice. That we will accept, but turn over your life to God? No way!

Then slowly we realize that it was our best thinking that got us here. Everybody had advice for us, but it didn't work.

That is when "surrendering" enters our mind, only when we know that we have failed.

He is a force that is so great, so magnificent,
so beyond our comprehension that we can only
accept or reject Him.

We can deny Him with will,
but that does not change Him.
He is still there, like it or not.

We can accept Him.
An acceptance that is based on love,
not comprehension.

You can love the ocean
without knowing everything about it.
You can love a person
without knowing how they think or feel
or be able to imitate them.

Thus it is with God
to surrender our will to His,
we do so with a faith, a trust,
not a knowing.

It is like being lead in the dark.
We can not see,
so we trust the person who can.
We move forward
not based upon what we know,
but trusting the leader.

Know that He is leading
and will lead you
for your own best interest
and that may not be
what you would choose,
but trusting Him
to choose for you.

It is your surrendering
in your admission of failure
that you ask for His help.
Keep placing your faith in him.

The more completely you can have faith,
the greater His power.

*Move and respond to each day with the Faith
that you are being lead correctly.*

*Do not fight what is happening,
do not criticize what is being done.
Just move in response to it,
without having to know where it is leading.*

*Put your Faith in God
allow Him to lead...and He will.*

*You must know that
He is not going to take over your life
and run it to your expectations,
but rather run it,
if you do not fight Him
to His expectation.
You cannot pick and chose
what you want it to be.*

Surrender means just that.
It is a grave responsibility.
It requires you to accept in faith
that He knows best and will be best.
You will not agree with Him at all times.
You may think you could do a better job.

But remember that it was in your
doing a better job that you created the
problems that you now have.

You must continue "giving up".
Your prayer to Him must say so,
over and over again.

Not for Him,
but to reassure you.

Remember this is not a stop and start situation.
You either do, or you do not.
Once committed,
you must stay committed.
Lukewarm is not good enough.

God will help you and lead you
for your own best interest.
He wants and desires to be needed by you.
He is God, but His pleasure comes from
helping those who need Him.

In helping them, He helps the world grow
into a better place for all of His loved ones.

Love is all, Love is God,
are terms you read in your books
and it is true.
God is a force of Love
and Love is giving,
caring and nurturing.

He gives all of this with pleasure
as you help your children.
You want to see them grow
and live in happiness.

So does He, for you are His child.

It is not an accident

that all the books of the world

call God the "Light" and "Father".

He has shown Himself to so many people

over the years in that form,

that it is not to be doubted.

He does want to be asked,

so that He does not interfere

with your free will.

He does not wish to impose Himself

any more than you wish

to impose your will on your children.

Their best interest comes first,

so you wait and watch them fight their problems.

Wanting to help, but not wanting to take away

their pride or initiative.

When your children tried, failed,
then needed your help
you gave it with pleasure of being able to help,
not with the pleasure of knowing they failed.

And thus it is with God.

He is love and intelligence.
He is all.
Trying to make Him fit into your
ability to comprehend Him,
is to limit Him in your mind.

He is so much more than you can know.
He exists in a realm beyond your knowledge,
beyond your comprehension.

Do not attempt to know Him intellectually.
You can not, simply accept Him.
Believe Him.

You cannot understand Him.

With the advent of drug abuse, alcohol abuse, child abuse, spousal abuse and our entertainment being almost limited to murder, mayhem and violence, the frequency of people taking their own life is beyond comprehension.

This letter was written as a direct result of a friend of mine, a mother of a teenage boy receiving a call at work saying that her son had just killed himself with a gun.

For a month she resumed her work and was seemingly untouched by the suicide. She read this Letter of the Soul with defiance, proud to be so strong. Yet once into the letter, the dam of her grief broke and she was able to acknowledge her pain.

She came to me the next morning without saying a word, put her arms around my waist, laid her head against my chest, held me for a long time and left without saying a word.

Tim's response to the question of suicide:

*It is not God, hell or the devil that punishes you. For there
is only God and he is love.*

*It is the soul itself that finds its own suicide
unacceptable.*

*Yes it knows the reason why it was done. It heard the
mental arguments that went on before.*

So it does have love and compassion for the person.

*Yet, for the person entering heaven there is a feeling of
failure, a job uncompleted, work yet to be done.*

The person will accept all the gifts of God.

*Yet, the feeling of one's not completed their job,
will drive the person to review and study their
life to seek and find the real and true reason
for the suicide.*

With that understanding the soul will try
to create the same condition
that led to it's failure again,
and if possible, with the same people.
When the stage is set, the soul will be reborn to the setting,
to try again to face the problems and win.

God knows of life's probes and He knows how difficult the
problems can be and He loves ever the losers, for He knows
that sooner or later they will all be winners.

It is in the battle with one's problems that the soul grows
and becomes strong.

Look at all of the truly great people in the world. Did they
have everything, no problems, or were they people that
overcame their lack and their problems, to succeed against
all odds?

It is these people that pull the world with them as they climb even higher.

Give your love to the person and grieve
not for their death, but only for your
personal loss, for they are not dead,
but are in GOD's Love and forgiveness.

*Have you noticed it is the small and frail men like Gandhi
that seem to move the world?*

*There is something about that weakness and courage that
becomes irresistible.*

*He was a man that could have succeeded
in becoming a small time lawyer, but he had a greatness
that would not allow it.*

*If the world would follow men like him, seek honor and
virtue and live by that standard, so much of the world's
problems would end.*

*Just think of how much pain and death is caused by man's
pride.*

*A set of standards that man could live by is so needed, to be
honest and caring, put other peoples needs above his wants.*

*Life is to be lived,
but not at the price
of other men's suffering.*

All forms of life have God in them.

They may not serve man,

but man does not serve them.

They have their development.

They have their learning and whether or not man

can appreciate them does not matter.

Man may be the highest in the mind of man.

That does not mean this it is true.

The way man is developing

shows that man is one of the least

successful of the species.

The fish and the insects were here before

and if man does not destroy the earth,

they will be here after man has killed himself.

You are going to be the dinosaurs of the future.

Bones to be found and wondered about.

Man must change himself if he is to survive.

He can change this world into a garden of Eden,

or into a garden of evil.

It is his choice.

Tim's Description of Himself.

As a person, I am a person of thought.
Just as, at times you live in your thoughts.

I do not have to care for my body
and physical needs as you do.
My time is spent in thoughts,
feelings, learning.

What to you is imagination,
is manifest in me, into my reality.

You live a combination of physical
thought and imagination.
Your thoughts and emotions are
at best, vague and ill defined.
Most of the time just a wisp of smoke
that is impossible to hold on to.

In spirit, these thoughts become
clear and strong and real.
We share your physical world
as well as your thoughts
and the thoughts of others
and the projected fulfillment
of those thoughts.

With this power of thought
we learn to control our thoughts,
otherwise our world would be in chaos.
We can create heaven or hell in a flash,
 the past or the future, just by changing our minds.

You have this ability, but it is mostly unused
and wasted. You are in the body
to learn the lesson of the body,
to learn how to take the problems of the body
and solve them.

You must face the hard facts of your life, take the responsibility. You must learn to solve your problems or fall before them.

*Though they can be harsh and cruel
at times, it is in problems that you
learn your strengths.*

*In my world there is a joint reality, cities,
land and organizations.*

*It is a joint effort of mutual
thought which is there when we need it,
though we rely upon it less and less.*

*We live in our thoughts and thoughts
of others and thoughts of God.*

*When we focus on God
we feel His ever enduring Love
and His knowledge.*

Rather like your going to a library
and once inside "knowing" all
the knowledge that is in all the books.
Hearing all the music and seeing
all the beauty at once.

We have friends,
but at a deeper level.
When we share our thoughts,
it is a sharing of everything, every detail,
a knowing that is above the limits
of your friendships.

We live a very full life.

About five years after Tim started writing through me, I felt another presence in my mind. Because I had accepted Tim's voice so freely, as a friend coming to call, I welcomed this new voice.

Though I heard no words, I did feel this need to draw. That in it's self would not have affected me. I do draw and paint. So the feeling was not strange. But the suddenness and strength of the feeling was great. I understood that it was from another entity. So I asked in my mind, "Is there someone here who wishes to draw?"

"YES I DO!"

JC: And who are you?

"MY NAME IS SAM".

JC: Do I know you?

SAM: "NO AND IT DOES NOT MATTER".

Please note the dominance and rudeness that are in the words. This was indeed another different person. I was amused.

SAM: *Just leave your hand free, and I will*

lead it...

(one page of loops followed...a long pause)

JC: Are you still here, Sam?

SAM: *Yes, I await you.*

JC: Please draw if you wish.

Are you learning to use my hand?

SAM: *Yes. It is not easy to learn what I*

must know to use you. It is hard.

JC: Name the subject you would like.

SAM: *To draw a bird in flight.*

(The drawings below are photo copies

of the actual drawing).

Aug. 1981

JC: Can you give me an image?

SAM: *Yes, you must first be quiet, then I will.*

(I "saw" in my mind. Mary holding the baby, Jesus in her arms, as though she was showing Him to the viewer. She is dressed in full length dark velvet blue royal gown with the head and neck white wrap that was used in Medieval times. She had a tall, high pointed crown on her head. Her background was black, with a circular stained-glass window to silhouette her. She was standing tall and proud.

The drawing below is just a sketch to remind me of the vision. I drew it, not Sam.

JC: Sam?   SAM: *Yes Jack, I am here.*

JC: How can I help you? (I was writing
       with a pencil)

SAM: *Use a pen rather than this pencil.*

JC: What art mediums do you use?

SAM: *My art was done in all mediums, pen,
       charcoal, paint and water, all things.
       But for now please allow me to learn
       your arm and hand.*

JC: Every time I feel you I think of New
       York City.

SAM: *Yes, in the late Thirties and Forties,
       and the place was Brooklyn.*

JC: Were you a successful artist?

SAM: *Yes, but only to a small degree. But,
       now that I am here I wish more than
       ever to draw, so the world can know
       the beauties of Heaven.*

JC: I "saw" a girl in a door. Your wife?

SAM: *Yes. You draw her face without
       feeling. She was filled with fun.
       Her arrival was the high point of
       my day.*

JC: Are we doing any good?

SAM: *No. It is your drawing, not mine. You*
        see my wife, but then you draw her,
        not me!

JC: There was not a thought in my mind

        that these drawings would ever be seen.

        They were done fast, not good.

        Simply to have a record of what I

        was "seeing" in my mind. I would "see"

        in a flash these images that were

        Sam's thought and Sam would move right

        on. Leaving me to keep up.

The vertical and horizontal lines that you will see in the background of some of the drawings are the lines of the secretarial pad that I was drawing on. Had I was known that they would be seen, I would have used more care.

SAM: *Let me show you more.*

JC: I saw nothing.

SAM: *You did see my thoughts, but you*
disregarded them.

The old fat woman was mine.

JC: Would you like me to
draw her?

JC:: O.K.?

SAM: *No. You did not give her*
the feeling of the housewife.

JC: Which is?

SAM: *The weight is heavy,*
the feet hurt and the brain is empty.

JC: I think I'm playing games.

SAM: *NO, YOU ARE NOT!!!*

JC: I tried again being careful not to override
       Sam's will,

JC: Is this yours?

SAM: *Yes, mine.*

Women of this
type filled my life
in Brooklyn. They
were on every street.
Going about their
life without a thought of change.
They were and that was all they knew.
Each married, raised their kids and went
into old age, not knowing that it
could be different.
My work was of the street
life of New York. Not
the glamour, but of the
daily life of the people.

JC: My mind is too full of thoughts
and pictures now. Tell me about
yourself, or your apartment.

SAM: *My best work was done about the people,*
life I knew best. I was born and raised
in New York City. It was the only thing
I know and thus art to me was showing
the New York I knew. I know that you
had a different life and New York
was strange to you, but to me it was
my Universe.

JC: What do you think of New York now?

SAM: *Oh, I don't like it. It was never a*
pretty place but now New York and
it's people have given up the human
race. Each person is afraid of the
other. The young feed off the old.
Homes are now jails, locked in, barred
in, with no hope of freedom.
Perhaps you and I can change it,
even if only to a small degree.

Oct. 18, 1982

JC: Sam, are you with me?

SAM: *Yes Jack, I saw you going though my*
drawings. Let us try to work again.
I understand the problem.

JC: Good, let us try to make our contact
stronger by writing. It is so weak
that I doubt it and yet when I look
at your drawings and your comments,
I know you are real.

SAM: *The world changes too fast and I*
feel I am being left behind. Your
work is good and perhaps through you
and people like you the world can
be changed. The world is too cruel,
people no longer care for one another.
Everywhere you look people are pushing
and shoving others aside. No longer
is there time for friendship, peace
or quiet, just rushing. If the world
does not stop its a mad race into
death, all will be lost.

Fill the river of hate up with boulders of Love and the river
changes course and mankind is saved.

JC: Sam gave me this thought.

SAM: *All over the world there are people that know*
        and see the harm, but we need to know that
        others do and see. Reach them and join them in their
        beliefs. When enough people are together and know
        the harm that is being
        done, then we will prevail and God's work
        will begin again.

        Try to go on, join other people, let our words
        and our art be seen. To convince one is to step
        closer to victory over darkness.

SAM: *First I want you to allow me to use your arm. It may take a while, but I must learn to use it. I can't possibly teach you with words, my art. It is a feeling that moves the spirit.*

(a man praying)

JC: Sam, was this yours or mine?

Sam: *It was mine. You realize that you had never drawn a picture with darkness.*

JC: (To explain. Sam had drawn only the shadows and what was left was the light, which formed the subject.) More?

Sam: *Yes, I have been waiting too long. not to want to keep going.*

JC: Should I keep my eyes open?

Sam: *Yes, I see through yours eyes.*

JC: This picture may not impress you, but it shocks
me.

First, I grew up in Delray Beach, Fla. A world of
Palm trees, blue tropical skies, beautiful clear blue
waters, boats, diving, sailing, etc. When I drew
anything, it was the life I knew.

Now here I am drawing tenement buildings and
the life style of the "Poor and Unknown", with the
help of a spirit I can't see and who is complaining
about a missing garbage can.

SAM: *This is the hall. It was always so*
dark and no lights were on.

Oct. 18, 1982

SAM: *Yes, this was my apartment. The room*
was our living room and the afternoon
sun was our only source of light and
warmth. But we lived there with each
other and made our life happy.
It was cold in the winter and hot in
the summer. It was all we knew and
thus our joy was in each other.

JC: I felt that there was something that should be under the window. It just didn't feel right, so I asked Sam.

SAM: *There was a long buffet table with a white lace cloth on it.*

JC: I am excited about what we are doing.

SAM: *So am I. It is so good to see my world again and there is so much more. I will be here. I am anxious to work. It has been too long, just quiet and allow my thoughts to come.*

JC: *I have never, would never, draw a*

picture of a cold, old woman sitting beside a

garbage can.

Sam using my hand, started with the hem line.
Using continuous lines, did the skirt. Then the
overcoat, shaping her body within the coat, the
cloche' the face the legs and shoes.

At this point I had a drawing of the woman
sitting, no, hanging in space. With that he indicated
the wall and sidewalk with a few fast stokes, then the
garbage can and at last, the chair.

All done in a matter of a few minutes.

SAM: *He was a friend of mine and fed me*
many times between pay checks.

JC: What is your critique on my drawing?

SAM: *You did not allow me to do as I wanted.*
The arm and hand are incorrect. The
face is good, but the body is too fat.

JC: I have never drawn a full face with style or
        personality. My effort would begin by
        drawing a oval, then dividing it with three
        light lines to show eyes, nose and chin.
        But this started with two bright dots that
        grew into eyes, then eye lids, eye brows into a
        full face, then head and hair. Marceled hair!

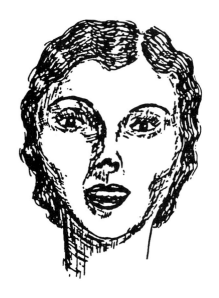

JC: I can't believe this!!!

SAM: It is true. That was my wife. It is so good
        to draw again and you are good at letting me.

JC: (Please note, a COMPLIMENT!!)

SAM: *I am as pleased about our work as you are. Please let's continue. Let me show you my thought. (a boy's face with dark cap and shadow across his face).*

SAM: *That was my Son, Jerome.*

JC: Would you like me to use a pencil?

SAM: *No, I know what I am doing if you just let me!*

JC: I felt "round the eyes".

SAM: *Yes, but use only the lightest of strokes.*

JC: Does the mouth need changing?

SAM: *Yes, but I don't know if we can.*

Sam drew this for me a few days ago (1996). It is his and Ruth's bedroom. Please note, the style of the furniture, the sink in the bathroom, the overhead light, the lack of windows. It was a "Cold water walk up" Brooklyn, in the 1930s.

I asked him what meaning it had for him and he replied: "Of Love, yes. But also of being too cold in the winter and too hot in the summer and of illnesses".

SAM: *Lets go to work.*

JC: I "saw" a boy, Jewish, lower than eye
       level, a cap and jacket. Sam using
       my hand, drew him.

SAM: *That's it. Jerome, when he was
       younger.*

JC: Was he your only child?

SAM: *Yes and the Light of my Life.*

JC: Tell me about your boy.

SAM: *He is about your age now. He still
       lives in Brooklyn. Like me, he never
       thinks of living any place else. He
       runs a small shop. He has two sons
       of his own.*

JC: Why did you choose that expression?

SAM: *He used to play outside in the streets,
       and it was hard to be Jewish in New
       York. There were always those that
       picked on him.*

Oct. 20, 1982

SAM: *My wife passed on after I died. We*
both died too young. New York takes
its toll on young people.

JC: Why did you love it?

SAM: *I don't know that I loved it. It was*
all I knew and the enemy known, is
better than the enemy unknown.

Jan. 8, 1983

SAM: *I know this is just the beginning.*
I could occupy all of your time with
my drawings. I have an eternity to
draw, but I know you do not, so I
will be patient.

(After two unsuccessful drawings, I
gave up. Please note that over a
year had passed since I had written
or drawn for Sam. I had tried, but
was unable to get anything worth
saving).

Jan. 9, 1983

SAM: *My art was everything to me... It was*
a shame that I did not do well
financially, for it inhibited my work.
To draw and capture some expression
or thought on paper was so important
to me. I could look back years later
and relive that experience. To express
myself through my art was so rewarding.
If only more people would try, it
does not matter if it is good or bad.
Just the joy of creating, of watching
a picture grow, of feeling the pride
of accomplishment is so rich.

JC: When we first spoke in our minds
to each other you said you sold your
work to the New Yorker Magazine. Later,
you said you did not. Please explain.

SAM: *You wanted something to identify with*
and the New Yorker did carry vignette
pictures and that was the kind of
pictures I drew. I wanted you to
understand my art.

*Let me teach you about myself. I was born and raised in
New York. Like so many Jews, I lived in a closed society.
Taught by Rabbis and raised by a typical Jewish mother.
My childhood was hard. The world appeared to be against
Jews. We felt hated and did not know why. Everywhere we
looked, we were aware that people distrusted us and
scorned us. It was hard and to survive we created an
attitude that protected us. Yet it was in this same attitude
that the seeds of hate were created.*

*To say that we are at fault is too easy. We certainly share
the blame, but this has been going on far too long for each
generation to be able to change.*

*The hate is there and the defense is there and they have to
be faced. It is like good and evil. Each person knows that
evil is wrong, but sees it only in other people while doing
the same and sees it as necessary.*

SAM, cont.

If the whole world could be stopped and each person recognize his or her responsibility in it, then change, the world would be a paradise. But it can not be done.

Each person in themselves must stop being judgmental and begin doing right themselves. Then slowly over a period of many centuries, when enough people are good and kind, the need to be defensive will decrease.

It is not only a problem of the Jews, but a problem of every person. Hate only creates hate and love creates love. It is a hard lesson, but it is the only lesson.

People see only the evil and ignore the good. Our people are the most generous of the faiths. In our giving, we support many charities, both Jewish and non-Jewish. We take care our own. We have many more homes for the elderly, than your faith does.

We prosper partly because we cooperate within our faith to promote the young and establish them in their careers.

Yes, I know we are dishonest by your
standards, yet how often do you hear of a Jewish mugger,
robber, or murderer?

Our criminals are of the white collar type
and unlawful things are done just inside the law. All in all,
I see little difference among our people. You do it one way
and we do it another. Neither are all right, or all wrong.

We, you and I, see the difference and ignore the
similarities. It is a vicious circle that revolves because two
play the game. When one stops playing, the wheel will slow
down and stop.

(This is perhaps the very best definition I have
ever read or heard of the conflict between our two
religions. It is so clear and rational that I cannot do
anything but accept it for its truth. I know with all of
my heart that I am incapable of writing it myself.)

JC: I often tried to write and draw for Sam. But
        most of the time, I could not receive him. So I
        would go years and not write. Then I received
        this.

SAM: *Every time you write or read my words,*
        I come to you, hoping that you will
        write more.

JC: (My son asked me to paint a sailboat
        at sea for his birthday. I did and
        was very proud of my work. It had color,
        excitement, drama. He liked it and
        hung it with pride.
        Then I made the mistake of asking
        Sam for his opinion.)

SAM: *You did well, but your colors were*
        too bright and the edging was not
        of the best, but all and all, it was
        O.K. He was pleased and that is all
        that matters. But next time, let me
        help you.

JC: (So, I went out and hung myself.)

*Being over here, if there is such a thing as "Over Here"
is fine. There is much to do and learn and see. Our world is
only limited by our imagination and mine is active. But
there is a quality about life that draws us back. A challenge
perhaps, or a memory of the good times. We think back and
do look in to see. But for the most part we would rather be
here than there.*

*Your world is becoming less with every passing day. The
mood of the people is sour, the outlook bleak.*

*Where as in my world of old, we were worse off than
now. But, we had hope and optimism. We knew things
were bad, but they were going to improve. Now your
young people feel that the good years have passed and the
world moves on into over crowding, more crime, more
violence, more distrust. That with rare exception, the world
will only grow darker.*

SAM:

"Being over here" is fine at first. It is too good to believe.
The glories and beauties of it are too good, too wonderful.
   After a while you begin to long for the realities of Earth.
To truly feel the cold, the work, the love. It is as though we
are protected here by GOD's Love and that prevents us
from knowing life.
   To be on Earth is hard, and at times cruel, but it has its
rewards, a Nitty Gritty feeling.

JC: Did I copy that right?

SAM: *Yes, that is what I wanted to say!*
          Bed is wonderful when you are cold
          and tired, but once you are rested
          and warmed you want to get up and
          be going about your day.

JC: It sounds like you are ready to be
          reborn, again.

SAM: *Yes, I think about it often now and*
          I am sure when the time is ripe,
          I will.

JC: When you come back, will it be in New York as a Jew?

SAM: *No, not there this time. Once around in New York is enough. There are other places a Jew can live.*

JC: Have all of your passed lives been as a Jew?

SAM: *No, but the past few have been. It is good and though you have problems, the rewards are worth it.*

JC: Such as?

SAM: *Having a wife that considers her role in life to be a wife and mother, or having a society that is close knit. It is good to know that you will always be accepted among your own. We are like strangers in a foreign country. You are friends, without question when you meet one of your own.*

SAM:

*I used to draw and paint for my living. It was not easy.
The people I knew and dealt with were usually poor, or if
not poor wanted as much work as possible for the least
amount of money.*

*The small businesses in my area were only interested in
paintings that would tell the buyer what they had to sell or
offer. They were just advertisements. No one was interested
in beauty or emotions. The times were too hard. The
appreciation of beauty was a luxury they could not afford.
So most of my good work was done for my pleasure, which
does not pay the rent.*

*Those little sketches that told a story or captured a
feeling were my favorites. The Grand Paintings were not
my style or reflective of my life. A street scene, a look and
emotion reflected on a face were my joy.*

SAM:

To me a picture should do so much more than just show the physical. A camera can do that. It is the feeling that counts.

Our area was poor, the life was hard and cruel and yet the people survived. They loved and laughed, were sick and healthy and they had courage. New York has a way of always defeating it's people and yet they always arose and went on to try again.

You could say they had no choice, but that is not to give them credit for their lifetime of fighting. For during it all they had time to love, marry, have children and go to their graves, fighting and loving and caring every inch of the way.

To capture this was my pleasure.

SAM's wife, RUTH

SAM: *My wife is here with me, watching*
everything. This is very exciting
to us. It is rare that we get to deal
directly with the living.

JC: Would she care to write?

SAM: *Yes she would and her name is Ruth.*

RUTH: *I am delighted to be here and share*
this. We on this side watch you the
living and wish we could reach you.
But it is difficult for ours thoughts
to be interpreted as your thoughts.
We live and learn, hoping to
influence the world, but we usually
cannot until we are reborn. Then
we often forget our good intentions.

JC: Sam had drawn your picture and you
are beautiful. It is obvious that
he loved you dearly.

RUTH: *Our life was good. It was hard and*
difficult, but our love for each other
kept us going.

RUTH:*Our boy was such a joy to us and it was hard*

seeing him hurt so by life. Now he is a man and

has sons of his own, so the cycle goes

round one more turn.

His sons may never know the life he had and

that is a blessing. There is just as much hate

now as before, but people do not show it.

Thus we are able to live with less fear.

We over here know what the world should

know, as a teacher knows the examination. But

we must keep quiet and allow you the living

to learn and find your way. We wish to help.

Our role is to watch and advise as we can, but to

step in and take over we can not do.

God, in His wisdom, knows that to learn a

lesson is to remember it. To be told the answer

is as nothing. Your work is a way we can reach

people and guide them to God.

When all look to God, then the world will

move into the Light and GOD's will, will be done.

Sept. 1995

I always question myself whether these drawing are mine or how much I may influence them. I really try not to, by holding myself as mentally passive as possible. But these two faces are totally different than I would have drawn.

My mental image of Sam was a lank, gaunt bearded Judaic, a Biblical classic. So it came as a complete shock when Sam drew himself the way he did. His hand moved fast and sure. I know that I had no part, except to hold the pencil for him.

My reaction was: "Is this for real??"

SAM replied, "*This is how I looked, not handsome, but adequate*".

My sister Dorothy, or Dot as the family called her, was an incredibly unique person full of contradictions, excitement, drive, ambition unlimited. Yet seemingly totally unaware of whole areas of human experience.

Dot was six years old when I was born. The first time Dot saw me she looked at me, then at Mother, and asked, "You are not going to keep him, are you?".

As an adult I was a foot taller then she. Even in public she would introduce me as her baby brother. She always found reason to threaten me and still does from the "other side", but always with love and fun.

Being brother and sister gave us a wonderful gift. We could be who we really were, not who we should be. We could agree or fight as we wanted and it did not interfere with our love for each other.

Though we sometimes went years of being apart, we were never separated. Not even in death. We continue to fight with love and she still picks on me, but that's what big sisters do.

Dot was wild, independent. She quit school when she was in the eighth grade to work as a secretary in a law office for $5.00 a week.

She married a sailor when she was 18, who went on to make a career of the Navy, retiring as a Commander.

During her life with him, she lived in Casablanca, and Rebote, French Morroco. There she learned French and an adequate use of the Arabic language.

With her use of the three languages and an absolute lust for adventure, the whole world was endangered.

She explored the Atlas Mountains in northern Sahara by herself in a Volkswagen. These mountains are a remote place where just being alive is a good reason to be killed.

Upon returning to the States they settled in Washington where she entered Real Estate. Soon after her husband and she were divorced.

Dot did the only logical thing. She became a millionaire. This included being on the Board of Directors of the bank that once had refused her credit because she was without a husband. I so pity the bank officer that had refused her. May he rest in peace.

Dot's second husband was a Lt. Colonel in the cavalry as well as top physicist. She seemed to have a thing for military men.

After his death, Dot traveled the world, even including teaching conversational English in a Chinese University.

When she married her third husband, a navy officer, she had met her match. He was a man who loved travel and adventure as much as she. They planned to live life in a high speed race, to do and feel everything. But it was not to be.

Shortly after their marriage, Dot's health began to decline. In just two years she went from nonstop energy and excitement to fatigue and loss of memory. She still fought to travel, but simply could not.

The painful side of Dot was her absolute fear of becoming old and helpless and not dying. She had a Living Will that spelled out all of the details and our promises to use it if and when the time came.

Dot did not believe in God. "How could a God allow all the pain in the world?". She "knew" that death was the end, everything else was wishful thinking.

Because I believe so strongly that He is a God of Love, a gentle Father, I tried to share my thoughts. The only concession I could get from her was that God "may" be a force of creativity.

Then on July 20, 1994, Dot was found on the floor unconscious. The Doctor upon examination said that Dot suffered a massive stroke and was not going to recover, or even regain consciousness.

She was going to die.

We exercised her "Living Will" and she was moved to a Hospice.

July 25, 1994

Dot was in a heavy coma and despite pain medication, she was groaning and moving. She looked as though she was in great pain. I asked Tim, "What can you tell me about Dot's condition?"

Tim, replied with absolute casualness and calmness,

"Dot is well and on this side."

TIM: *"She visits herself when you are there". She no longer is in the body and she says that "You were right about the passing. IT WAS GLORIOUS, AND WHAT A RELIEF!."*

JC: Can she speak to me now, or is it too soon?

TIM: *"No, she is here and tells me to speak for her. She wishes you love, and tell her husband that he was her Great Love. She hated to leave him, but the body would not go on. She fell and that was all she could remember. She saw the effort you all made and she loves you for it, but she was free and happy again. Death holds no mysteries. It was a quiet passing, even if the body is still alive, it is without her.*

Your mother and father were there to meet her, and it was a grand reunion.

TIM: *She is glad to be free of the body and it's problems and to tell her husband she loves him and will keep an eye on him. That he is to pursue his happiness now, knowing that she is with him.*

All is well and will be in the future.

Her body will die soon, but it is no longer her."

JC: Of course I felt loss with Dot's passing. She had been an important part of my life. But in this contact I knew that she would continue to be with me. She had feared living sick and old. Now that was behind her and she was "FREE" again, as Dot should be. That made me happy for her. Dot's body may be dead, but Dot was very much alive.

Today Dot began to write though me. This means that I heard her voice speaking in my mind. I would write down each word one at a time, not knowing what the thought was or where it was going.

These first writings were of a Love Letter to her husband. A letter that was so personal and so beautiful that I, nor any other man could have written it. The words were from a woman to her husband. So Loving, so knowing, that they could only come from the person that had lived the marriage.

Upon finishing the letter, she showed me (I saw in my mind, her thought) a beautiful, pale pink rose.

Knowing that he would not be home, I placed the letter, crossed by a single pale pink rose on their bed.

The letter was so beautiful that I wanted to read it to someone else. She agreed, but after I had read it, she asked me not to do it again. It was just too personal. I had to agree, even though I would have liked to include it here. I can not.

From this point on Dot wrote to me freely and gladly, but often writing about personal issues that I am not including here. So the thoughts may be inclined to jump around a bit.

July 31,1994

JC: Welcome Dot--You are an Angel, now!

DOT: *Oh, far from it. Wings do not become me.*
But it is Heaven. It is impossible to describe. Everything is yours, before you know you want it,
to think is to have, dreams fulfilled in a flash, colors, music, views, beyond the human knowledge. Life, the highest of the high.

DOT: *This is the true reality and life in body is*
       a life of labor and doubts. (I "saw" a salt mine,)
       It is only to strengthen the spirit, to learn
       lessons that can not be taught here, where
       everything is pleasure and joy.

       Tell Jim, (her husband) I am with him all the
       time, that he is my focus. Tell him not to give
       up on me or dwell in my loss, but rather to
       keep loving me and see me though the eyes of
       the heart, to know that I am with him, but I just
       stepped out of the room and will be right back.
       No need to even miss me.

{To Jim}: *You can not think of me, that I do not know*
       it. So talk to me, love me with yours words for
       I can hear and know that my love is for you.
       Allow yourself to feel and hear.

       When Jim received my letter and the rose, he
       was overwhelmed, dubious, questioning, not
       fully accepting, yet wishing to believe, touched,
       but still doubtful. "He will question you".

JC: How have you found our mother and father?

DOT: *Quite different from the people we knew. You do not take over all of the personality. So don't expect to meet the same person, but rather to meet a more profound and thoughtful person. Perhaps the person they could have been if time and situation had been different.*

JC: Do you understand them better than you did?

DOT: *Yes, it is as though the people now, were acting a role of what they thought they were supposed to be. Doing the best they could in that time and space. They were learning the soul's lesson too, just as you are now.*

JC: Dot always had a cat. She always named them "Pistol". Now I realize that it was their independence she loved and "Pistol" expressed that quality. So today when I asked Dot, "What else can you tell me about the "life" of Dot?

DOT: *"Oh, She was a pistol. I was full of ideas and drive. I wanted to get things done, NOW! I was so filled with inner excitement and impatience. Tomorrow would be too late. In fact my impatience came over with me."*

JC: God help Heaven!

DOT: *I'm selling Real Estate over here. "Want to buy a lot"? (I passed.) I tried to always do my best, but I somehow seemed, always, to be out of step. You were a total mystery to me. You were always so calm and quiet, even if things happened to you. They never seemed to touch you.*

Sept. 1, 1996

DOT: *My illness was horrible. My loss of*
       independence killed me. Needing others
       to look after me was hard. Being weak and
       without memory was painful. So death was
       wished for.
       When it came, I found myself watching all of
       you working over me. I stayed with you most
       of the day. You were so concerned and yet
       there was no need to fear, for I was well and
       happy.

JC: Tell me about your life now.

DOT: *It is easy, it is wonderful. We have and see*
       everything we want. I have met with our
       Mother and Father and with many of my
       friends, that I used to know.
       It isn't so much that we "see" them as it is that
       we "know" them. Yes we see the form, but
       not as we used to see, but rather the essence of
       them. The good without the bad, the joy
       without the sadness.

Sept.4, 1994

DOT: *It is strange that within the body*
       you never know what people think, but
       once out of body, minds open up and all is
       known. We do not infringe with our ability,
       but when thoughts concern us, we know.

JC: What else have you learned over there?

DOT: *That all things needed are available. If you only*
       would see, Love, knowledge, wealth, everything
       is there. It is as you say, not a case of learning
       rather putting aside the restriction that you pick
       up in a lifetime. Just as you found and thus live
       in beauty. Everything else is there.

       You (speaking of all living) accept and
       surround yourself with walls, barriers,
       and limitations that are not wanted or
       needed.

Sept. 4, 1994, cont.

DOT: *Even your language restricts you to a*
particular way of seeing, thinking.
You think that life makes gaining wealth
hard, when in reality everything wants you
to succeed. There are banks, organizations that
look for winners to make them wealthy.
People just waiting to join your band wagon.
Don't think for a moment that I made my
money by myself. No way!

You told me that God was a creative force. It is
true. All things come together in Him and are
expanded, changed, developed and
represented. Much as an artist, in all that he
has known, creates a new, developed and
changed thought, so it is with God.
In the beginning, if there was a beginning,
GOD's palette was limited. From one thought
became two, one reality, became his palette to
add too, develop, try and sometimes fail.

cont.

Now, His palette, His universe and His colors are rich beyond belief and you could say His medium is life.

Not just man, but all Life grows, multiplies, spreads, develops, changes, follows every path and becomes incredibly complex and richer with every passing moment. Man unfortunately thinks that he is the highest and the closest to God, but that is only man's ego. When in reality, the entire universe is His life. Even that, is unknown to you.

The universe that you know is limited to what you know and in reality, expands ever outward growing larger and smaller beyond your comprehension. It is not limited to just the physical, but also to the nonphysical.

It could be said that there are universes of sound (just ask any great musician), colors, light, dark and forces that exist only in energies and the energies of energies.

cont.

*You have just discovered the DNA. All of the life, power
and direction of "you"is hidden in an invisible speck of
liquid that is in every cell of your body.*

*It is possible for you to know the DNA, say it,
but never to understand it.*

*Your world has just discovered the electromagnetic field
in this 100 years and you use it for your computers, light,
TV etc.*

*Yet that power has always existed and does exist in
everything, everywhere and mostly you are blind to it, with
only your most learned, gaining the simplest of
understanding.*

*You live and limit your knowledge to a three
dimensional world. Yet with the quickest of thought, you
know there are endless dimensions. You speak of time and
measure it in the past, the present and the future. Yet, this
very concept limits your knowledge.*

DOT, cont.

Because everything you know has a beginning and an end, you feel that even nothingness, if there is such a thing, has to end. If it did what would be beyond it?

That your own abilities and life must have an end.

Yet, I am proof that it does not.

You are a thousand unread books, a million unaccomplished, accomplishments. You complain that you can't fulfill your needs and yet the whole world is yours, for the taking.

If you would just see.

Sept. 9, 1994

DOT: "*It must seem strange to you that someone who did not belief in anything could become so outspoken, so believing in a month.*

It was with excited disbelief that the whole concept of heaven, God, eternal life, opened to me. From that first moment I found myself out of my body, knowing that I was dead (or would soon be) and yet fully alive and actually joyous knowing that I was free of that old and helpless body.

Being pulled away and yet going back to watch and being pulled away again.

Going to the light with full joy and understanding, thanks to you. Being received by all, as a returning traveler would be.

Surrounded by Mother and Dad and many others that you would not know. Welcomed and loved, not so much as "Dorothy", but rather the person I really am. Shown views, thoughts, in a rapid fire of excitement as when people all talk at one time.

Knowing that I was home and had just been away for too long, but home again".

Sept.6, 1994

DOT: "*Tell everyone that Death is the return to real life and that life is but a play acted out on a stage of your choice.*

That no matter how real and painful you may think it is, you are just an actor fulfilling a role. A role that's purpose is to strengthen you for the next play.

Life is very real and can be painful and horrible, yet it is a play that you have chosen because it teaches you those lessons you need to know.

The horrors of Germany were indeed horrible, but the people that suffered the most are the most strong now, filled with strength and courage and love and compassion.

No one ever developed these traits by comfort and plenty.

It deepens your colors and makes you prepared to fight harder, to prevent it from happening again.

Yes, it does go on, we have a history of horrors and will continue to have as long as men place their greed above human life.

DOT: *Will it come to an end? Yes, for the spirits, but the stage of life will play for a long time, until all know what it is that's wrong.*

JC: What of punishment by God?

DOT: *As punishment everywhere, it would only*
     fulfill the need to be cruel and
     it is but an extension of cruelty,
     not an end to it.

JC: How can man fight cruelty without
        setting punishment of those that
        are cruel?

DOT: *The very words belie themselves.*
     The answer is to establish a society
     that is so cooperative and loving that
     no one would violate the peace.

     I know this sounds idealistic and
     impractical, but is your way working?

DOT: *That does not mean the criminal should be let free. No. Society must protect itself from the rogue. But, prisons should be a place of learning, counseling, mental and spiritual study.*

With the criminal being released only when, and if, he has changed and does so fully and completely when the lessons are learned.

I know this is difficult and for the wild mind it would be punishment. In the long run, it would work and cost society far less in money, time and crime.

Rather than doing nothing for punishment, or hard work, or torture. A prisoner would be taught a profitable career, learn subjects that open his mind and soul, classes that would teach him to deal with people from a view point of cooperation and mutual trust.

Sept. 7, 1994

JC: I am so impressed!!! Eight pages of
beautiful, Spiritual thoughts just
37 days after your passing. I can't
believe your growth.

When you were in body, your thoughts
and actions lead me to think that
you were an infant soul (meaning,
living and seeing only the material
world and reacting to it with desire
and control).

But now I am hearing so much growth
that I know I was wrong. Can you explain
this to me?

DOT: *Yes Jack, the soul often takes on*
journeys for the purpose of learning.
Much as a scholar would go back to
kindergarten for a chance to see life
anew, to try the growing process from
a beginning perspective.

JC: I have a friend who is an adult child of a verbally abusive mother. I asked Dot what she would advise and this is was her answer. It is also good advice to anyone caught in that unhappy trap.

DOT: *"Everyone has someone that has affected their lives negatively, it goes with the job.*

It is in the overcoming of that, the lesson lies.

In the looking for the strength within, to put off that cloak of doubt and shame, that you find in your life.

You can never change the person, you can only change yourself. You can never change the past, only the future. Measure your own worth and move forward with that knowledge.

Make your life happy and full of life, loving yourself and others. Then the other person you left behind and their strength becomes less with each of your personal victories. When you can sympathy for them you have succeeded.

DOT: *There are always new things to learn and to grow is to move upwards into a rarefied world, until you reach a point of being isolated from your roots.*

My life was a great lesson. I learned how to expect more from others, as well as myself, to create a life that was not extraordinary, to start without anything and nobody and give life hell. Find fun, excitement, travel, success all by myself.

It was a life worth living. I loved it!

You are in a position now to put aside the needs of life and go out and teach, write, speak.
Christ, you are not. But you can and must, reach many.

Sept. 8, 1994

Dot and I were "discussing" GOD's revenge and punishment.

DOT: *It is difficult not to think of revenge. Yet it serves only the purpose of making the person want his revenge. Revenge "works" only if you kill or break the person.*

But when you do not have death or hell, then the problem is answered by Love. Not love in the simple fawning type, but in the caring, nurturing support way.

Once the evil person is on our side, they know the harm they have done. They see and feel the pain they have inflicted. They have the mirror of their lives shown to them.

If there has to be a punishment, then this is it. They now have to work through their sins step by step. Knowing what they did and knowing what they could have done, seeing the world they created and the world they could have created.

You do not punish the insane, the drunk, the weak minded, if you did it would only serve to make you the evil one.

Sept. 8, 1994 cont.

DOT: *St. Paul killed, tortured, yet, awoke from his*
evilness and became a champion of love.

Some of the most accomplished people on your earth
learned to love and serve by having lives of evil.

Look at the number of people dedicating their lives to the
service of men in AA, NA etc. People that go into prisons
to work with the criminals.

If we had killed or broke those people when they were in
their evil, would it have served a purpose?

The Soul is a part of God and God is only Love and a
life of eternity.

There are evil men who have souls, but the man in his
life can be evil, regardless of what his Soul should want. As
an evil man can have loving, kind, gentle parents that are
horrified by what their child does. The Soul does feel the
shame and does learn from the evil.

JC: You were always such a worrier for
women and against men. Yet, you refer
to God in the masculine.

DOT: *Only to talk to you. We must use the
language that is understood.*

JC: Is there a gender in the Soul?

DOT: *No, that exists only in the body and
has no place here.*

*The soul is as a teacher. The soul
goes with the person. Living the life
with them and yet, not being in
control. It tries to teach, gives advice
hoping the person will learn. But,
as there are good teachers that do
change the lives of the people and
poor teachers that cannot influence
the people that they are helping.*

JC: Then in each evil person is a good
soul trying to correct, but is unable
to change their person?

DOT: *Yes.*

Sept. 9,1994

JC: This morning I was watching a TV show
about animals. Do you wish to instruct
me on animals and our spiritual
relationship with them and their
spiritual knowledge?

DOT: *This is a problem in that animals*
are still in the instinctual level.
Though the doors are opening to them.
Still most of their lives and thoughts
are automatic. Yes, they love their
young and each other and this is
part of their growth. When animals
live with loving humans, (as your cats)
they move up the ladder and they do
affect us spiritually.

But to say they are spiritual is
pushing their level beyond reality.
They love and grieve and have sympathy,
and if you wish to see it as spiritual,
I guess it does no harm.

Sept. 15, 1994

DOT: *Know that God is beyond your comprehension. He is far too vast, far too old in time, far too complex to be within your reach. But know that He is here and without Him you would not be.*

Don't take this to mean that you should not love Him and seek to understand Him. It is in this that you grow. Don't expect any answers that will bring Him into your intelligent comprehension...

A bird may fly, but will never understand aerodynamics. God is a force of life. It is in His energy that you have yours. It is in His intelligence that your are. It is in His Love that you find yours.

He is all, everything that is, is God. You, your world, life, knowledge are all parts and a very small part, of God. You can not be separate and apart from God. You may not believe in Him, but that is your error. You are, and you are of God, and God Loves you".

Sept. 15, 1994, cont'

DOT: *"When mankind can understand that, then it will awaken from it's slumber. Man sees himself as so high, so important, that he feels God is just a step above Him. As though God is just the next step up.*

All of which proves how little man knows of God and how little he knows of himself.

Your teaching is how you will serve God.

JC: Thank you Dot. I am still in amazement. How I wish you were this open when you were alive.

DOT: *Yes Jack, so do I, but I had to be "Dot", to reach this plane.*

Sept. 16, 1994

(Her death plus 26 days)

JC: Good Morning Dot. I just reread yesterday's writing with disbelief. You have blossomed into a teacher!

DOT: *And I have more for you. I just heard you think of reincarnation. It is true, perhaps not exactly as you know it, but the difference is important.*

Yes, you do live many lives. How else could you reach this complex person you are without a background of a history of lives? You are born in a new body, but as soon as that baby is ready then a steady flow of knowledge descends to teach the baby how to do even the simplest of tasks. That in themselves are incredibly complex.

What man calls instinct is in reality the knowledge of the soul. That comes not from the experienced learning of this new body, but the learned experience of many, many life times dating back to the creation of life.

JC: Good Morning, my Sainted Sister.

DOT: "*Good Morning Jack and thanks for your raise in rank, but I am still am your big sister and don't you forget it!*

Once we learn that life is forever, we can begin to relax and enjoy our lives. Once the fear of death is taken away, life can go on, a learning lesson with ultimately no failure.

We all must come again and again, for it serves us well. Where else can a spirit explore all possibilities of life. To fail and win, to be bad and to be good is the lesson to learn for ourselves, the lessons needed to know.

Life is very real to those who do not understand that life is eternal. Once we know that, rather than live in fear, we are free to feel and learn and love. A blessing that is sometimes too hard, but we always win".

Sept. 29, 1994

JC: Good Morning Dot. I can see why you were
        a success. You see life as a battle to be
        won, whereas I see it as a lesson to be
        enjoyed. What could I have done or said
        to have introduced you to Spirituality?

DOT: *Probably nothing. As you see our lives were*
        so different. My success and your lack of
        it was my proof that I was right. If you
        had succeeded, I would have listened.
        Otherwise, no.

JC: Good answer. Where do I end and you begin?
        How much do you influence me without my
        knowledge? How much are you unable to
        influence me?

DOT: *I think you heard my answer before you wrote*
        the question. I am as a friend that is by
        your side, not all the time, as life is filled with
        uneventful times, but at times of retrospect or
        action. I am there as a conversational friend,
        unable to do anything, but just to talk with you.
        This includes times when you are not
        knowledgeable of my person.

Sept. 29, 1994 cont.

We can not alter things or acts, only give advice. Whether or not it is heard. Yes, there are occasional things we can do, symbols that you can recognize. But all in all you must live your life and we can only observe and offer advice and as in friendship, often advice is not welcome or heard.

DOT: *Can you harm anyone?*

JC: No

DOT: *Can you lie or be unfaithful?*

JC: No.

DOT: *Does not the problems of the world lie in these two acts?*

JC: Dot, I feel we have a book here. (This is the first moment that I thought of writing a book about and for Dot).

DOT: *"I hope so, we are working together at such a close level that is filled with emotions and fun and by the way, we spirits are capable of feeling emotions both good and bad.*

Oct. 1. 1994

DOT: *For all of Tim's writings you were*
never able to think of him as an
emotional soul, but rather with a
profound awe that put him above feelings
and ego".

JC: Now that I am writing with you, how
does Tim feel about it?

DOT: *"He is glad, for your "do nothing"*
was and is, a pain to deal with .
So he welcomes the chance to turn it
over to someone with more clout!"

JC: You are too much, Dot.

DOT: *Today's lesson is Love. I know Tim*
has spoken so often about it, but I
must add my 2 bits. (a 1930's term
meaning 25 cents)
Perhaps nothing is so needed and is so lacking,
as Love.
All of the problems of the world, which are
profound, could be answered if everyone gave
respect and love.

Oct. 1, 1994

DOT: *Each person should treat themselves, their family, their neighbors, their people and all people with Love.*

To create an environment where there's less than, then above would not be acceptable.

The problems of the world with food, water, land, all have answers. In fact, if man would just leave the world alone rather then trying to change it, the world would heal itself and so would man.

Man does not have to control other men to be successful. Mutual cooperation would be far more productive.

Teach this lesson Jack, for it applies to everyone, every person, the people in your group, as well as the murders in Uganda.

For each person has a level of anger that really serves no purpose, except to separate them from others.

JC: I know that in life you believed in suicide. Do you still?

DOT: *"Yes I do, though I know it is not acceptable, nevertheless, a horrible death gains nothing.*
I know that it is a blemish on the soul, but I would accept that, rather than suffer hideously.

God does love and forgives and I'll let Him".

JC: Who else would say that....except DOT? That's my sister.
What other things over there surprises you?

DOT: *"That it even exists". I had expected just not to be, Zero. But there is a world of life here and all of a sudden it makes sense.*
Why should all of this history be fulfilled in just one lifetime. We did not get where we are in the learning of just one life. We are an accumulation of the learning of many lifetimes.

Life does go on almost uninterrupted. It is in this that we truly grow, and learn, and serve.

DOT: *We see God not as a person, or an omnipotent human, but rather as a Love, an omnipotent knowing that exceeds everything we can possible know".*

Just as you cannot comprehend the ocean or the Universe, know that those things are just a small part of Him. That he is the total of everything and as Tim says "and more". Any attempt to humanize Him, to see Him as a man, is just man's inability to comprehend the incomprehensible.

If man could only accept Him and love Him and live his life as a devotion to Him, man, all men, the whole world and God would be pleased and better off.

It is, as you say, "so simple". Man has always instinctually known what he should do and yet finds every reason not to do it.

Why is this so difficult?

Oct. 3, 1994, cont.

JC: How are you doing on a personal level?
     Getting enough to eat? Still going to bed
     at 6 PM?

DOT: *Life here is different from there. Without the body*
and it's needs the mind and soul are free to pursue it's own
ends.

    You can never know there what it is like. Life without
the needs of the body. How much time is spent meeting the
needs of the body.

    With that gone you are free, truly free to explore who
you really are, to see back and ahead in time, to know all of
the reaches of the soul, to have, feel and share all of your
own complexes.

    Somehow, I have to compare it with music. The full
range and color of music is without end and varies with
each person. To reach for and not find the end of your life is
exhilarating.

Oct. 9, 1994

JC: This was written one beautiful morning while sitting on the dock. Good Morning Dot, I feel as though I am in paradise now. The Sun, Sky, Water, the cat, the water teeming with fish, the coolness, the warmth.

I feel that this is God and that I am a part of God. That this is what God means.

DOT: *"You are right, God is found in all of life and beauty. He is in everything that is not of man's making. But if it is alive and beautiful, it is a symbol of God, His hand work, His Love expressed. Imagine, what the world would be like if man allowed GOD's beauty to exist? If man honored GOD's work, Man would prosper far more. His cities would not ugly the land, man would work in a positive world. Living and making his living with nature, rather than killing it"*.

Oct. 9, 1994

JC: How does this compare with your home
        (heaven) at this moment?

DOT: *The same, but your day will change.*
        You have things to do that will be
        less than this. But Heaven is this.
        The mood, the joy, you can feel now
        is continuous.

JC: People speak of churches, schools,
        ranks, and levels, in heaven. I have
        trouble with this.

DOT: *You are right, Heaven is a state of*
        mind. Those human things are created
        by those that come over, but they soon
        realize that the spirit has no need
        for the physical. Why buildings? We
        have no bad weather. Why rank? We have
        no ego. We love and appreciate, but
        that does not bestow rank.
        We all function at the best of our ability and it
        is appreciated. It is one of peace, joy, beauty and
        an awareness of God as the basis of everything
        that they represent.

Oct. 24, 1994

DOT: *Your day has started well, I envy you, your life as compared with the life I led. You seem to be so content, so appreciative of all things, not seeking to change them, but to enjoy them. That was not true of my life. I was always seeking, needing more than I had.*

Yes, I did many exciting and wonderful things, things most people never do and yet I was always left with a hunger for more. It was as though I was always hungry. Eating all I wanted, yet staying hungry. Where you seem to be always happily full. This is a lesson worth teaching".

JC: I have been thinking of our Mother a great deal since you and I are talking on such a intimate level.

DOT: *She is here and shares most of our conversations.*

JC: I know that in many ways I have disappointed
        her and that grieves me, but I also think she
        must be pleased with the overall package.

DOT: *Yes, she is. She loves you and watches out for*
        you. She knows you and your problems.

JC: Does she (my Mother) wish to speak with me?

DOT: *Yes she does.*

JC: This is a surprise. I had not expected that my
        Mother would be able to come through after
        nine years. My Mother and I had been very
        close all of my life. We were very important to
        each other. After a five year illness and pain,
        She died at the age of 88, in 1986.

Thirteen days later she came to me. She told me of her passing, of her experience with the Light of Love and the meeting with her loved ones on the otherside. We wrote together for months, but slowly the writings came to an end.

JC: Welcome Mother, I miss you.

MOTHER (Laura):...*And I miss you, even though I know of you and often look in on you. You are my most important person. Do not fear that I have lost my love for you. That could never happen. As you love your children despite what they may have done you kept right on loving them. This is how it is with me.*

MOTHER: *There is so much to teach and so much to say and yet the words do not tell the story.*

JC: Do you plan to reincarnate?

MOTHER: *Not for a while. Time is not of*
importance here. There you watch every
year. Here we are. And as long as we are
content and learning we do not desire physical
life. There will come a time when the class
must began again, but now I feel no draw
toward the physical.

JC: You are a Great, Great Grandmother now.

MOTHER: *Yes, so I heard and they are all beautiful in*
spirit as in body. The Great Granddaughters
are so far removed from Earth it will be a joy
watching them develop. Give them my love
and tell them I watch over them. The
emotional side of life seems to stay with the
body. The strength of the soul, the essences of
it, comes over. The trivial, the mundane, dies
with you.

JC: I am so pleased to talk with you again.
          The older I become, the more I see your
          mark on me and it pleases me. I love you.

MOTHER: *I love you.*

Nov. 1, 1994

JC: You say that I don't really understand
reincarnation. Please tell me.

DOT: *"You see life in a physical reality and that
reality has to have time and a physical body.
When in reality it is far more of metaphysical
reality. Try to understand that the soul is not
the size and shape of the body, nor does it
have to have the physical life of the body.
Without the restrictions of the body it can do
things, be things, that a body cannot.
You dream and in your dreams you have a reality
that is far from perfect. It is enough to cause
you to laugh, have sex and have fear.
For those moments that is your reality. Yet,
where is it? What is it?
It is a metaphysical reality. Real in the human
sense, but not in hard physical reality. Yet, real
to you.*

DOT: *It could be said that the physical life is a dream of*
          the soul or a joint reality formed by many souls. It
          does not meet the standard of hard reality if it were
          not a dream".

JC: Wow, Dot, that is heavy!

JC: Could it be said that pure thought is the
          greatest reality?

DOT: *God is the greatest reality, for He is all. It is man's*
          inability to grasp, that weakens what men
          perceive.

          Man is on the pathway to becoming God or at
          least, to join God, everything else is to prepare
          man for the job.

          As eternity is timeless, man's trip to God is
          timeless. Man, in his impatience, tries to
          become God in his one life. Yet, man has
          difficulty enough controlling his own life
          much less control all there is.

          Man is a small part of God. He is capable of
          reason, creativity, decisions, yet, he has
          difficult enough just coping.

DOT: *So, the lesson has to be taken over and over again.*
In all times and in all situations, going from infancy to old
age in both sexes hopefully gaining a little bit with each
step.

There will be a time in all lives when man sees life for
what it is, an illusion and then he is free to continue his
studies without the obstacle of living when the physical
gives way to thought, which changes to spirit. Then that
spirit develops into joining with GOD's spirit and fuels
GOD's Love.

December 1994

JC: Today, I had lunch with two of Dot's friends.

JC: Did you join us today?

DOT: *Yes I did and it was good seeing my old friends*
again.
I heard you say I was there with them and I was. It is
a shame I could not speak to them. But somehow I
think it is necessary for them to find me within
themselves.

DOT: *We do not want to force or expose ourselves. The dead are suppose to leave life behind. Never to be a part of it again. The living should only know the life there and to be suspect of life here.*

If it becomes too proven, too acceptable, they will give up their lifetime duties. The lesson left unanswered becomes fuel for their self learning. To give too many answers, to be too obvious, is to take away the learning process. It would do no good to give the students the answers to the test. They would not study.

People like you pursue the knowledge until you understand. In doing so, you need to teach. Not enough to give away all the answers, but enough to create curiosity in your students.

Spirituality enforced,
does not replace,
Spirituality learned.

Feb.26, 1995

JC: Good Morning Dot. I have just read your past writings and I am still amazed at your increased growth and your understanding.

DOT: *"Thank you Jack. I know as I grow how little I saw of the world around me. I never understood how people thought. It was as though all people were strangers. They all had their own problems, their own fears, that I could not see. It as though we were actors on a stage, each reading from a script, saying their lines, but not feeling them.*

It is only when you get past the script, that the real person is found. When you drop your script and they do the same, can you really get to know someone.

Then and only then, can you experience and love the other person. Until then, love itself, is a script.

JC: That was GOOD!!

DOT: *You have so much to give and I am*
just beginning to appreciate it. For the years you have left,
pursue this personal contact.

Make plans for your group and teach them
how this belief can transcend into personal
life. It is not just an abstract idea, but
is appropriate to any and all situations.
In this concept it is joy and peace to live your life. It can
give them the answers to many of their problems and an
overview and perspective of life. Often people feel totally
out of control and at the mercy of others and of life itself.

With this belief, they can see the patterns
of life and their role in life. Living this way, life's mundane
problems are seen as a simple thing to do. They have no
affect on their lives, whereas the joys of life are magnified.
No lives are immune from this and all can be helped.
To walk through life focusing on it's beauty and joy,
is to have a life that is worth living and is a fulfillment.

These are the final pages. It is not all there is, for this represents only about five percent of what I have received with more added almost daily.

Anytime I want to talk with my friends, they are there for me, always ready to answer my questions and advise me.

This is available to you. But you have to ask and then listen, they will speak with you. This will come quickly for some and others may have no response at all. If there is a secret, it is in only learning to quiet your own mind.

Most people are victims of their minds. Their mind races, worries, changes from one subject to another, non-stop. In reality, you can control your mind just as you control your own hands, feet, mouth. Just as a young child can run wild, if not controlled. Your mind must be controlled if you are to live a full, productive life.

This can be done by prayer or meditation. I do not mean ritualistic, formal, speaking by rote, though this can be effective for some. I am speaking of anything that creates quietness in you physically, emotionally and mentally.

It is in this state of quietness that you will find the real you, your inner peace, your spirituality and your personal health, emotionally and physically.

It is your choice.

IT IS YOUR CHOICE.....

( )   To embrace the wisdom and teachings of
        Love and Peace, that are expressed by
        the real authors of "Letters" and share
        them with everyone.

( )   The above, plus be a part of the
        Spiritual Quest Network and receive
        future "Letters" by writing your name
        and address below. No cost.

( )   The above, plus submit your writings
        or Channeled writings for consideration
        for publication in Spiritual Quest
        Newsletters, mailed monthly.
        Year subscription $24.00.

( )   The above, plus, create a monthly
        meeting for your friends, to share
        this interest in the Spiritual, to
        discuss the lessons of this book and
        the monthly newsletter and all
        related subjects.

( )   Having done the above, create more
        groups to continue what you have
        accomplished. Speak to groups on
        radio talk shows, teaching the Spiritual
        Quest lessons to classes, with income
        for you, from classes and speaking fees.

( )   I choose to check my area of interest
        and request further information and
        details WITHOUT OBLIGATION.

Name: Please print

Address

City   State   Zip

Spiritual Quest, 308 Teqesta Drive. Suite 20
Tequesta, Florida. 33469

Arthur

Barbara Harris Whitfield tells of her very unique Near Death Experience, that changed her whole life, from a wife and mother, to a researcher in the medical sciences. Speaking at universities, hospitals, churches, and as a guest of the top television shows. In "FULL CIRCLE" (Pocket Books, 1990) Barbara Harris reveals her incredible life from the personal perspective, with profound insights.

"SPIRITUAL AWAKENING" is an account of Barbara's research at the University of Connecticut Medical School, The International Association of Near Death Studies and her own personal discoveries. Barbara has been a guest on Larry King Live, Oprah. The Today Show, and she has been published in Redbook, Psychology Today, and many other shows and magazines. To meet this gifted, and interesting lady, be sure to read her books. You could only be richer for it.

To purchase Barbara's books, just call
        1-800-441-5569

"LETTERS OF THE SOUL", makes a perfect gift for someone who is on their own personal Spiritual Quest.

LETTERS OF THE SOUL, $11.95 plus shipping.

If desired, this book can be "signed" by the author, gift wrapped and sent first class, for $20. Include a short note or card to the receiver. For this service, call (561) 745-2220, or order by mail. Please include your check, and the full name and address of the receiver.

Spiritual Quest Newsletter, 12 Issues $24.

ORDER FORM

Full Refund, without questions.
Mail Orders:
Spiritual Quest
308 Tequesta Drive, Suite 20
Tequesta, Florida, 33469

Name...

Address...

City.......................State.........Zip..............
Please include your check.

Fax Orders. (561) 745-2253
Ph. Order, call collect (561) 745-2220
Credit Card Orders. 1-800-879-4214
Please have your card ready.

THANK YOU